THE MORNING AFTER

Poetry and Prose
in a Post-Truth World

THE MORNING AFTER

Poetry and Prose
in a Post-Truth World

Margaret Randall

San Antonio, Texas
2017

First Edition

ISBN: 978-1-60940-540-3 (paperback original)

E-books:

ePub: 978-1-60940-541-0
Mobipocket/Kindle: 978-1-60940-542-7
Library PDF: 978-1-60940-543-4

Wings Press
627 E. Guenther
San Antonio, Texas 78210
Phone/fax: (210) 271-7805
On-line catalogue and ordering:
www.wingspress.com

Wings Press books are distributed to the trade by
Independent Publishers Group
www.ipgbook.com

Library of Congress Cataloging-in-Publication Data:

Names: Randall, Margaret, 1936- author.
Title: The morning after : poetry and prose in a post-truth
world / Margaret
  Randall.
Description: First edition. | San Antonio, Tex. : Wings
Press, 2017. |
  Includes bibliographical references.
Identifiers: LCCN 2017004477| ISBN 9781609405403
(pbk. : alk. paper) | ISBN 9781609405427 (kindle/mobi-
pocket ebook) | ISBN 9781609405434 (library pdf)

LCC PS3535.A56277 A6 2017
DDC 811/.54--dc23
LC record available at https://lccn.loc.gov/2017004477

This book is for Michele Frank

Contents

THE MORNING AFTER

Poetry and Prose
in a Post-Truth World

Hologram

The art of being wise is knowing what to overlook.
—William James

A flash of light. Not white. Nor black. Colorless as outer space and raging as those fiery lava spills fleeing their own terror, running and then coagulating and weaving themselves into ropes of new land, balanced above the depths.

Caught between centuries, interstices of time, rivulets of memory and energies that speed and slow as if their talents for sustaining whole belief systems depend upon a precise set of words or acts, this place has made itself scarce. Does it want to be found? Does it want me to find it, get to know its doubts, misgivings, egregious failures?

Some mornings I wake to its palm-studded beaches and distant mountain silhouette. Empty of beings. Then there are evenings, just before sleep, when crowds fill my eyes, all looking in the same direction, listening to the same voice. I cannot make out its coastline for the multitudes.

My questions are always some version of these: Where does imagined time meet experiential time? Where does the border of imagined space sidle up to the borders of those places we have been, and how do these borders come together, knit themselves around our cells, take up residence in corporeal memory?

Cosmologist Stephen Hawking tells us time travel is possible in one direction only. Forward. We cannot go back. Albert Einstein's theory of relativity shows us how more or less gravity makes it possible for us to travel through space and then return to a time that is days (or years or generations) after the moment of departure. We would have gone out and come back having altered our relationship to what we left behind.

Imagine going on a space flight, visiting a distant planet, and returning to earth. The people we loved have aged, died, and their descendants aged and died—so that you, the traveler, have been away for a few years at most, while generations have passed on earth. According to this same scientific assumption (law?), it is not possible for us to visit an earlier moment in history. That is the stuff of science fiction—fiction after all.

As a child I had trouble with corners, never knowing exactly where the dividing line was or how it spoke to me. Just as it was difficult for me then to understand how red and green traffic lights allowed both cars and those of us on foot to move in a well-controlled dance—I asked my father repeatedly, until his explanation suddenly clicked into my ability to comprehend his words—, I haven't been able to totally follow Hawking's logic; its fuzzy edges tease my readiness, leak elusive questions that scatter certainties and promises in equal measure.

Once I glimpsed the lines of a ruined citadel: a tall arch with blocks of stone fallen at its base. Then I fixated on a small yellow flower, growing from the rubble. Its delicate petals filled my frame, eliminating every surround. Voices silenced: a choreography of wordless mouths, moving. These two moments happened in the same place at the same time. I can no longer remember which I noticed first or how that which I saw later bore the imprint of my earlier gaze.

My shy place is so small it fits in the hollow of one hand, threatens to slip between my fingers. But it may grow without warning, engulfing me in its size, flattening me against a wall of my own construction, a wall of questions pushing me away from myself. The hologram and I spar with one another. When things begin to get serious, one of us loosens her grip and laughs. It's usually but not always the hologram.

As I age, time acquires unexpected properties. It may drag itself out or move to condense more quickly. I have become suspicious of its loyalty. This has nothing to do with patience, but requires something like patience to inhabit it with grace.

Age, implacable, is no hologram. Or is it? Experiencing its march is like opening a book whose pages remain uncut. Text mocks or reassures from within a secret cave. Wonder tinges its mouth.

I close my eyes. Form and content settle into a miniature space. I open them and the map expands, lifts, flies.

Will my hidden place's colors always be this bright?

Can I count on intuition, tradition, breadcrumbs, scent?

Would I even be wondering about something this insistent if it didn't exist?

I gather myself slowly, draw a hot bath, brush my teeth making sure to dedicate two full minutes to the task, equally divided between quadrants. Mottled skin offers dark spots of age and flaccid hanging folds. Eyes squint in unconvinced recognition. I lay clean clothes out: the old Levis and black sweater. Bare feet have always carried me from here to there, flat shoes if I must leave the house or navigate rough terrain.

Promises replace themselves in rapid succession. From sample size to much too large to swallow. From vast to intimate.

Color always speaks first, carrying me on its wings.

These days I think before releasing the words. No interruptions allowed.

A man, any man, proclaims himself righteous. Or others agree and kneel. The perfect scenario for business. Greed and profit always at the ready. Followers arrive, just a few at first, then millions. Great temples are built in the man's honor, surrounded by hovels where the faithful also turn their eyes toward the man and his convincing lies. Demands score a win at every level. Look up and bow down. A promise of other worlds. Money flows in a single direction, and power radiates from its pinnacle like lava exploding from the volcano's throat.

I stare up at the Golden Ratio, its proportion towering in graceful balance above the Parthenon's nearest column. At Petra I catch another glimpse. At Angkor Wat, a masturbating monkey crowds me as I rest upon a low wall; he too is tired, lazy in the afternoon heat. At the library/brothel of Ephesus the same monkey mysteriously appears once more. We become friends. The wooden planks and palm thatch of a humble *bohío* in Cuba's Pinar del Río make their best efforts to stand alongside such majestic marble and sandstone. Pride enables its success.

But radiance is in the eye of the beholder.

The half-standing walls of the Triumvirato sugar mill, signal the place where Carlota wanted freedom enough to risk her life. Eighteen forty-three. Nineteen seventy-five. One hundred thirty-two years separate that failed slave rebellion from the operation named for her—Carlota—when Cubans returned to Africa in a gesture meant to make amends for their ancestors' sins. The act collapses time, gives it wings, at some unexpected moment reverses the terrifying history.

We might call this a Day of Atonement. But most humans have found it easier to stage ritual than embody risk. At best, Truth and Reconciliation commissions, where survivors may bear witness, sometimes look their victimizers in the eye, ask for a justice that cannot erase their memory's horror or bring back their dead. They provide the narrowest of pathways, upon which decompression may occur. Like the woven line extending to the edge of a Navajo rug, through which the rug's spirit may wander free. Our great religions promise a better life after death. The belief itself suffers from its inability to grasp the teachings of Einstein, Hawking or that which our eyes see.

The T-shaped doorway used by our Ancestral Puebloans flexes its shoulders, shrinks to fit the map, and hides beneath the descending lid of my right eye.

In memory there is no up or down, only endless holograms of imagination.

Hiding in Millennial Wait

For years I've looked for myself in ancient walls
—Palenque, Banteay Srei, Kiet Seel—
searched for their stories on my skin and mine on theirs.

In collapse today, the baths at Perge still promise
afternoons where questions move
through water's healing dance.

New walls too, their angles grabbing my hands
or shouting *Go home,*
you are not wanted here.

Granite V of unforgotten names, Twin Towers
a hologram now, and all the border walls
separating us from ourselves.

Rapa Nui's accidental coast remains a puzzle.
At times I am sure mine were the legs
straining to pull stone figures

many times my weight to platforms where
they contemplate the waves.
Other times, familiar as my childhood yard

with its Victory Garden and ugly orange threat,
I turn a degree and know against all logic
—even memory's fiercest burn—

that I am the *moai* itself: one encrusted eye
still staring from its socket, the other
long fallen: hiding in millennial wait.

Turning East

Earth, that solid ball beneath our feet
spins in the vastness of space
where neither up nor down exists,
while on the orbital plane
of all we see and feel
our home on its axis tilts 23.5 degrees.

In directionless space, the tilt is only a tilt
in relationship to which
disproven theory?
Angled away from where?
Astronomers make discoveries
and poets ask questions.

This news already makes us dizzy,
then science informs us
the North Pole turned east in the year 2000.
Fifteen earth years traveling down
an alternate road. Veering
toward epiphany or emptiness?

Space has no up or down. Yet the Pole
reversed its drift from west to east,
shifted 75 degrees, a phenomenon
caused by melting ice sheets,
loss of water mass,
depletion of aquifers and drought.

What's more, fossil records give us
a history in which both poles
have begun a reversal
that happens every millennia.

This is the earth's interior magma
spinning us away from ourselves.

We catch fire, a civilization lured by the greed
we call progress, mirage
keeping change or solution beyond our reach.
The words fade, refocus, then fall
into place in perfect lockstep
with every savage lie.

No up, no down, no earthly cause for concern.
Yet this poet knows there is
a tipping point, a broken armature
dislodging equilibrium.
Our axis strays and the Compass Rose
falls off the picture plane.

Benoit Sees the Shapes

A quiet moment, yet we continue to marvel at its elegance.
Amused, Euclid laments no longer possessing
the breath to emit a joyous gasp.
He recognizes his smooth cones and spheres
have grown rough edges,
dance into ever smaller fingers reaching for the promised land.

Benoit Mandelbrot remembers the moment that changed his life
and ours. I saw how the shapes came together, he says,
(emphasis on saw), knows our language of words
cannot describe that other language he traces
until he shows us clouds and leaves,
shorelines and sand dunes chewed by wind and rain.

I love you, you tell me and no limits stalk our reckoning
as our fingers trace a line
between flesh and knowledge,
cellular memory and this field:
we are at once here and everywhere,
ancient patterns blooming on our skin.

To glimpse, see, then be able to teach draws wonder
from the heart while images of dying children
capture each nightly news cycle
and weapon-grade anything refuses to go down
in the history books as progress, only a sad detour
hastening our journey to that place of no return.

I want to trust Benoit's magical moment, Euclid's sanity,
Frida's double helix as I take your fingers into my heart
and hold them against our age.

I want to forget the contest itself leads to oblivion
and end this poem in hope
even as the evidence tries to stare me down.

The Theory that Swallows Its Tail

The theory of gravity we currently believe
distributes time like cards
while all eyes at the table
call themselves space
and strain to glimpse those concealed hands.

A world of time and space, yet experts
construct their theories
within those elements—
something like using a single body's heat
to weigh the essence of love.

And so our master theory swallows its own tail.
To describe reality, we must go
beyond reality. The ordinary laws of physics
operate within time, thus cannot explain
the beginning of time,

leaving the door open to those who trade
in superstition,
create their churches of dogma:
bully priests and circuses of followers
relegating thought to sketchy promise.

We wonder about a no-resuscitation order
in Jerusalem 33 CE, how many apples
fell from Newton's tree
or how high his imagination soared
before he pronounced his Second Law.

A bounty of virgins, ashes to ashes, or ashes
to nothingness, death-defying atoms
born again as something else.
Where and when carry equal weight
in the poet's imagination.

The theory swallows its tail, requiring
two fingers down the throat
or patience enough
to know those not yet born
will have something new to say.

Perhaps and Maybe

—For Bob Holman

I woke this morning thinking about two words: PERHAPS and MAYBE. They bobbed behind my half-closed eyes, outlined in thick Rouault-like black lines. Twins, but not identical. The first is cool and collected. If it had a color, it would be blue, or a tasteful blue-green. Of course it does have a color. All words, letters, sounds and numbers have colors to me.

My off-the-top-of-my-head definition of PERHAPS is to introduce a sliver of uncertainty into a statement, as in "perhaps I will finish the job today," while at the same time leaving little doubt that the job will get done, giving me some wiggle room I guess. Intention dressed in elegance, calm around the edges.

MAYBE, on the other hand, is candy-cane red. Commonplace. Teasing, taunting. "Yes, no, maybe so." Like the ditty or song a child might sing while skipping rope or playing jacks or hopscotch. "Are you going to tell her today?" "Well, maybe." You know no more now than before you asked the question.

Adverbs aren't as powerful as nouns or verbs. Whole languages exist without them, and you could probably make yourself understood in a desperate attempt to speak another's language without ever using one. Adverbs signal degree rather than action or event. No one would call them necessary, or even exciting.

The online New Oxford American Dictionary defines PERHAPS as "used to express uncertainty or possibility: *perhaps I should have been frank with him.* Used when one does not wish to be too definite or assertive in the expression of an opinion." You hold the opinion, no question about that. But don't be too threatening in the way you put it out there. The first example given is: *perhaps not surprisingly, he was cautious about committing himself.* Perhaps not surprisingly: an ambiguous way of saying something if ever there was one. Used when making a polite request, offer, or suggestion: *would you perhaps consent to act as our guide?* In other words, more about form than content. Haltingly superfluous.

The same dictionary defines MAYBE more straightforwardly: "Perhaps; possibly: *maybe I won't go back \ maybe she'd been wrong to accept this job."* Also lists it as a noun: *no ifs, buts, or maybes.*

Both words date to late Middle English, fifteenth century or so.

Faced with a job prospect, marriage proposal or offer of food when hungry, it's unlikely you'll hear a response involving either word. Yes would be expected. Or no in either of the first two cases if that's appropriate.

In some cultures, hospitality questions—particularly those regarding the offering of food—must be responded to negatively at least twice before politely accepting. A custom designed to prevent the taker from appearing overly eager. Just as the guest is obligated to refuse, the host or hostess is obliged to insist, until the requisite back and forth has run its course.

In other cultures, questions are asked that may seem strange or insulting to outsiders. In Vietnam, for example, at first meeting women are interrogated as to age and how many children they have. Any response is acceptable, except that childlessness is considered sad.

Online information is meant to be condensed, reduced to minimal expression like the emoticons and 144-character tweets so rapidly taking over mainstream communication. So I decide to dig deeper. The Compact Oxford English Dictionary (COED, New Edition, 1991) is a compendium of words and definitions assembled in such minuscule type you can only read it with the aid of the powerful magnifying glass sold with it. Each book page is composed of nine smaller pages and each of these has three columns. Slightly more than halfway through the volume (book page 1310, small page 548), five paragraphs are devoted to PERHAPS.

After telling us it is an adverb, and explaining that in vulgar or careless speech the word has often been shortened to p'raps, it informs us that it appears only three times in the Bible of 1612, all in the New Testament and all in the Rhemish version. That's the thing about going to scholarly source texts: you are encouraged to do more research, in this case find out what makes the Bible of 1612 a reference, and what Rhemish is. Turns out, there was no Bible of 1612. Sixteen eleven is the year in which the King James version of the Bible was written, and it was published that year. Rhemish refers to the French city of Reims, a location that played an important role in Christian political history.

Perhaps without meaning to, this entry also reveals COED's bias: toward Western Christian civilization. The dictionary doesn't situate its word origins by referencing Muslim or Buddhist texts, or tell us the equivalents in cultures such as Aztec or Khmer. Think about it. And about how we are shaped by where we come from and where we go with our questions.

Only after getting these bits of information out

of the way, does COED inform us that PERHAPS is "a word qualifying a statement so as to express possibility with uncertainty." Possibility with uncertainty. Now I know why I have been drawn to the word, with its perfect balance between what is possible and what may or may not happen. It is up to me, or you, to make it happen. Or keep it from happening. Either way, our will is involved.

Life's exquisite challenge.

Further down the column of infinitesimal print, definition B is worth quoting in full: "A statement qualified by 'perhaps,' an expression of possibility combined with uncertainty, suspicion, or doubt; an avowedly doubtful statement." Now suspicion has been added to uncertainty and our perfect balance has been pushed to cliff's edge. It has become a mystery, subject to the vagaries of chance or unknown forces. I am beginning to understand it is these hidden meanings folded into the word PERHAPS that give it its allure, much like the images half-obscured within the glyphs we see and that so firmly grab our imagination on Mayan stone. What is folded within something else. What speaks to us from beneath the surface. What will never let us believe we know it all.

On COED's page 1051 (small page 503), stuck between may-apple and may-bug, the word may-be or MAYBE is also listed as an adverb. Definition A refers us to "possibly, perhaps." Before assuming this is all I get, I read further and discover it is "sometimes used as a conjunction with a dependent *that*." And, more interestingly, that it is also common in the phrase "And I don't mean maybe." In other words: I am positive, sure. This arrogance may be MAYBE'S principle claim to fame.

In fact, after these dictionary definitions I am ready to explore what PERHAPS and MAYBE mean to me, why I opened my eyes this morning with both words clamoring for attention, begging to be taken seriously. It must be about choice, I think, the way I have always fought for options and emphasized, with other women in particular, how limiting it will be if we accept at face value only those which society offers us.

It will be of primary importance, I tell younger women especially, to understand there are other choices: more than you can imagine, unexpected, strange-looking, surprising. Choices that may not fit neatly with the expectations you have been taught to believe are inevitable. The best evidence against ideas involving fate or destiny.

Play with dolls or construction sets. Go with protocol or with your feelings. Let that boy kiss you or resign yourself to being an outcast. Or, let that girl kiss you. Or kiss her. Find a man or remain what the patriarchy disdainfully calls a spinster. You're your body inside or outside the marriage contract. Identify as male or female or anyone else along our human arc. Be a mother and an artist. Sell out or not sell at all. Go to war or let them destroy us. Make a profit or save the planet. Forget or remember. Grow old and stay young, accepting both conditions joyously.

Any child, given the freedom to explore her instincts will come up with dozens of alternative equations, rejecting the confines of our binary world. Perhaps this is the real difference between cyberspeak and human-speak: we are made of more than zeroes and ones.

Words

Have we moved beyond word time, beyond the poet's terrain
where words describe events or pull us into new orbits
of wonder and release?

Words: those beautiful evocations strung together to birth ideas,
whispered as comfort, sung as praise,
perhaps even change the world.

The Divine Word has long since fallen into disrepute.
Words of judges and advertisers fail miserably,
bully promises groveling at our feet.

A lifetime creating monuments of words, and today
I have none with the power to evoke or heal:
sad yearning for new tools.

The words *strength, courage* and *love* recoil on this map
drawn by power's ugly hand.
Where have their radiant colors gone?

No territorial defense is worth a single child's death.
No empire justifies this crazed race to bigger,
biggest, best—and then oblivion.

No word justifies hunger, war, advanced technology
wreaking devastation on the innocent.
No word at all.

Has poetry come to the end of the line or will we keep on
making new things: resist retreat shaped like capitulation,
our love blooming like spring?

Words. Numbers. Pictures. Distance.

Words felled by backlog stagger off tongues,
break from mouths
into an empty space now numbed to shock.
Words like *terror, loss, why,*
forfeit their ability
to stand where we feel.

Words like *gay, Hispanic* and *Muslim*
only get in the way.
Orlando and *Ataturk*
stretch our map
but place us beyond its crumbling edge.

In the wake of this failure, numbers take a shot:
41 at the airport, 49 in the gay dance club,
20 school children, 6 teachers, 43
who would have been teachers,
their bodies burned and hidden
by men in suited power.

Five unarmed black boys, 5 white police: do these
fives
hold a different weight in us,
their wives' bereavement
or children's loss
a different pain?

Pictures step in to try their hand
—worth a thousand—
those final minutes
on a dying cell phone,

last message tweeted home,
notes, flowers, and teddy bears
swelling the newest memorial.

Color crouches beyond the mind's borders,
memorizing itself
upon a future
that may not arrive in time,
memorials barely visible
in rained out distance.

Words, numbers, pictures no longer work
and color only consoles in a future tense.
Safe from the viscous stench of death
we are at a fatal remove.
Imminent threat fades to worn rhetoric.
Life at the edge goes on.
Them and *us* is not an answer
that can stop the madness, loss,
descent into the rupture of post-history.

I Call My Words Poem

I use words, those given me in childhood
in starched suburbia, shot through
with mother's dreams of cruel refinement
and father's common lexicon:
colors changing on an artist's palette.

Later my words emerged from wind-swept sand,
among cholla, mesquite and dung beetle tracks,
inventing an alternate universe
against teenage conformity and Cold War fear,
bullied but fleeing imprisonment.

Creating my own, I call my words poem,
reshaping those I inherited
or unearthed, store them in secret places,
sometimes forgetting their power
to take me home.

Entering my ninth decade, I sort my words
by shape and weight, catalogue them
according to that old color code,
display them by relevance
to personal passion, collective need.

I pick up one whose mother was Miskito,
sister *la Malinche* of Mexican infamy
or fame, brother a martyr of any revolution
meant to be sung in the perfect pitch
of a Vietnamese field where water buffalo graze.

I turn it in hand and want to know if it will
prove equal to the task required now,
rocked with terror, woven of lies,
if it can breach a horizon
never ready for its threat.

My job is to arrange my words so they
will spell dignity and solace,
produce strong offspring
able to endure the exhausting struggle
of a return to reason and compassion,

creativity, integrity and love:
qualities that will keep them
breathing through generations
of newly minted language that tells
the battle-weary story of our lives

.

The Translation Project

Written after selecting the poets and their
poems, writing the introduction and
translating the texts for *Only the Road /
Solo el camino: Eight Decades of Cuban Poetry*

First I chose the poets, then their poems.
The map where I walked grew
transparent then dense as Precambrian rock.
It was winter but the words themselves
stumbled across thresholds
carrying the weightlessness
of spring.

The silvery-blue number fourteen loomed
until its one and its four
switched places,
danced close to slow music
then abandoned themselves
to the rhythms of *cumbia*
and *guaguancó*.

A door opened revealing another door
and another, mixed metaphors
dissolving in smoky mirrors
where images collapse
beneath the weight
of so many questions.
I follow every one.

Where I huddled with him and all his tribe
only her truth was audible.
Words flew in from another century
and I deciphered their porcelain music

ignoring dirty blankets
seeded with an invisible danger
I knew could do me in.

Her voice discharged its hormones
in three-quarter time
and I found them piled behind a door
unopened for fifty years.
You, standing beside
this pillar of salt,
threatened to take my last breath.

You over there fought me until, exhausted,
I gave up and let you have your way.
Half the foreseeable future was Royal palms
and a coastline pretending to be
wall or direction
battered by strange creatures
bearing guns and shields.

I dissembled her wit and his suicide gasp,
then rebuilt each in its register,
refusing to let them sleep.
Her quiet irony, his broken rage,
your last line and the silence
between your syllables
echo only themselves.

Their ears hold another language now,
identical yet entirely different,
recognize legacy
as their mouths emit strange sounds
where readers from a country
none of them know
pay homage to perfect pitch.

Translation After All

We trip over language, revel in the spoken word
and wonder about origins, who is distinguished
by its use and who less human
lacking its finesse.

The *big brain-small brain* thing serves as explanation.
But isn't it ironic we of the tiniest computer chips
insist large brains are needed
for cognition?

Suddenly a linguist informs us it's not language but grammar
raises humankind above the other mammals,
combining words the skill
that sets us apart.

I wonder then how we might hear the silence between barks,
bugle calls, growls, whistles, trills and grunts,
how many discrete phrases a whale sends
through its darkness of singing seas.

Imprisoned within an image of self that admits no rival,
we measure sound with our own poor ears,
spend billions on gaping receptor dishes
listening to the universe.

Unable to fathom others' language except through ours,
we may be polished in our speech
but arrogance and failed imagination
keep us from translation.

Theory to Prophecy

Every theory is a self-fulfilling prophecy
that orders experience
into the framework it provides.
—Ruth Hubbard

Prophecy to framework,
power unleashed
will take us from one failure
to the next:
a blade with two sharp edges.

As long as power is the prize,
failure will be its suit
of emperor's new clothes:
tricking only the greedy,
never those they devour.

Fire burned the hand that lit its grace,
agriculture always had hunger
in its sight,
progress walks on bound feet
and war never ended war.

The weary poem shows us
where we've been
and where we may go,
gifting us imagination
for the courage to choose another course.

A Relevant Question

Cuba with air conditioning and food
is the way some exiles
describe Miami:
six words that underwrite
personal decision
twitching in political defense.

Blowing over ninety miles of serene
or choppy sea,
ferocious winds roared
through the broken windows
of our ninth-story balcony:
illusion to some, torment to others.

Plantains and yucca, mango and rice
may not offer the variety
of Miami's Biltmore dining room
but are foods grown
by hands that sustain
a dream defying exhaustion.

Each mirror chooses its history,
octave or fifth.
A relevant question may be:
does mathematics describe reality
or is reality the Fibonacci sequence
of our confused desire?

A Nameless Distinction

—For Silvia Gil

When shame invades the beach
which rocks harbor relief?
We've gotta get by, he says,
spelling a nameless distinction.
Where does truth hide
in a jungle of lies?
How did hope fade
as horizons disappeared?

We wanted to build something new:
justice and equality
in the bully's back yard.
Promise donned an invisible suit
and we ignored its frayed hem,
worn collar and uniform buttons.

Forget the past, they urged,
and look to the future.
Then they opened the door.
A new era was proclaimed.
But no one could breathe the air
on an Island lapped by sea
and false promises.

Few memories remained
of those fertile years,
mangoes heavy on the branch,
possibility on every tongue.

The Neo-Fascist State

Road parts ways with rage,
stands proud
as it invites us on mysterious journeys,
shows us perspective
disappearing in distance.
Place or noun: keeping us safe
or dead.

Road rage: metaphor and threat
common in this petulant time,
hiding its nature in decibels
or camouflage, always dependent
upon the relationship
between ear and commanding voice.

My cells remember every movement
caught in time's accounting,
groomed by invisible teeth,
pretending possession of my body
as I send smoke signals of resistance
to the four directions.

The Only Adequate War Memorial

Veteran Ehren Tool makes small ceramic cups as a way
of dignifying the pain of those surviving battle.
He says peace is the only adequate war memorial.

Time isn't the hiker she once was, struggles
on the uphill, hurts for breath
when Juniper pollen
floats on hazy springtime air.

They keep tinkering with the clocks,
Spring Forward and Fall Back
reminding us direction insists upon
improving expedient living.

But whose expediency? I will spring
forward until I no longer can,
then fall back onto a bed
of my singular making.

Cushioned by tired words, their sounds
dulled by use, faces ready
to take up residence
in younger eyes, cracked mirrors.

Springing and falling better left to the artist
who listens to the rhythms of hunger
and heart, knows peace is
the only adequate war memorial.

Time wearies of pomp and circumstance,
respectfully folded flags, pink blossoms
falling through every season
onto perfection of identical cold white slabs.

Keep tinkering with the clocks if you must,
if you think it makes a difference,
keep upping the ante
until there is no one left to bury.

Just One Day's News

in a single paper of record: Pope Francis
above the centerfold
urges less judgment but cannot find an equal place
for women in his church, accepts
queers though refuses to honor our love.
Be more tolerant, he says,
but tradition lords it over change.
The exclusive club adjusts its discourse,
not its heart.

Presidential contenders lie across every divide,
kiss babies, faux acknowledgment
to those who strain their necks for greeting.
The hopefuls pounce on rival vulnerability
and move in for the kill, counting on
the money machine and promise of favor
to win them votes
in a system that doesn't yet recognize
one each.

We savor the terrorist's every childhood dream,
his mother cannot imagine, her baby
would never. Neighbors are shocked,
nothing but pleasant good mornings:
only the ritual comings and goings
expected in these times,
while the agencies we trust to keep us safe
guard their jealous secrets:
patriotic collars, spit-polish boots.

Eighteen-year-old model in petulant pose
wins the Instagram game and helps sell
$700 T-shirts. Everyone loves him,
the article says, everyone wants to be him,
while millions in unhip shirts
flee today's wars, helpless shadows
pushed to barbwire borders
then sucked back like human waste
for the next political speech.

Language fights itself, what once meant up
is now down, and reason is suspect
as ice melts beneath the feet of polar bears,
it snows on an August desert
and burns the last vestige of hope
where swollen eyes and bellies
draw our attention to a thrashing
of helpless limbs: stories
that cannot risk the truth.

Just one day's news on one front page.
We may choose to
keep our subscription current
or decide it's all too much
for blood pressure
carefully controlled
by the latest prescription miracle
designed to cure
a recently-named disease.

Call and Response

Standing before Jonathas de Andrade's
art piece Race and Class at the SITE Santa Fe
biennial "New Perspectives on the Art
of the Americas: Much Wider than a Line,"
September, 2016.

People engaged in response
to photographer's call,
taking the camera on,
taking on the viewer,
taking on themselves.

Don't you end up like them,
a mother tells her son,
driving past crack houses
on a street that remembers
perfect lawns.

Read about the savages.
Hey, don't scalp me,
she says,
trading slapstick for hurt,
crooked smile catching its breath.

Sharp-edged syllables crouch
in her blue eyes,
ride the tilt of his broad nose,
take cover in that halo of hair
then pay the toll to exit her lips.

They shatter the surface
of this conversation
when we ask the questions

hidden by silence,
broken in shame.

Class is the house being built,
race the house in ruins.
Here they are one and the same.
You there, tell me your story.
And you and you.

Questions brave danger
in search of answers
riding another's memory,
homing like pigeons
in the dark.

I Cannot Speak for the Gun

I cannot speak for the gun
doing its ugly job
in George Zimmerman's overeager hands.
I cannot speak for those eighteen ounces
easily concealed in a killer's pocket.

Easy to guess what George's intention was,
too easy to imagine the terror
in Trayvon's eyes,
the grief his mother holds
years beyond her loss.

The Law never found Zimmerman guilty
or condemned his crime.
And Martin could not know
his death would bring a nation
into the streets

or that hundreds of other black youth
would have to die, gunned down
by white policemen
or self-styled protectors
of an order that runs by exception

in this country where Law protects
the men who write it, works
for white, fails for black, rich
or poor, genders
that matter or don't.

Now George Zimmerman auctions
the gun that murdered

Trayvon Martin. He's asking
$5,000, promises some of the money
will go to fight Black Lives Matter

because, simply put, they don't matter
to him. Will this gun's new home
turn its barrel around
or lure another trigger finger
in wait?

I cannot speak for the gun or the men
who love caressing its fever.
My job is finding the words
that describe the weapon's threat
precisely.

Younger than that Now

I was so much older then. I'm younger than that now.
—Bob Dylan, "My Back Pages," 1964

Great hands holding seasonal scales
rise and fall
as they are touched by babies' births
old clocks and spring rains.

A gaggle of tiny Peregrine mouths open
to mother's repurposed offering,
crowd the nest
perched high above our hope.

Hope fades when we forget such scenes,
revives when memory paints them
in vivid color, malleable tense.
No politician's rant can take their place.

Younger than that now, I am ready to use
this image saved from ruin.
Older then, I almost missed
its promise.

Animals

—For my grandson, Daniel

The buffalo come to Standing Rock,
covering offended earth
with their hulking presence.
They bring memory of other times
when animals shared a human place.

Men and women, some on horseback
(and here they shoot horses too)
stand up to SWAT teams, tanks
and German Shepherds
harnessed to attack.

Species with guns conquer those without.
Species without become
what humans use them for.
Balance turns its back on justice
in wind's competing directions.

These dogs remind us of the roles
dogs were forced to play
in Birmingham, 1963:
trained to be beasts
at the hands of savages.

At Standing Rock the people cry out
against an oil pipeline
threatening land, water,
air in which life
may speak its whole name.

The buffalo settle in dry grass
along the broad Missouri.
When they keen their history's song
who will decipher
their language?

A Good Day

A good day for Aleppo's
six-year-old
when last night's bombs
missed that part of her building
still standing among rubble
and vanishing memories.

A good day for the Black father
in his car, waiting
to pick his daughter up from school
when every over-eager
trigger-hungry cop
is busy somewhere else.

A good day for the nuclear plant worker
when his shift ends
without a disaster in the cooling system,
no release of radioactivity
erasing those family photos
of his childhood dreams.

A good day for Kate when her husband
doesn't make it home,
allowing her bruises to fade
before the next time
she tells herself won't come
if she can just stop making him so mad.

A good day for the hungry man
with the cardboard sign,
he has $37,

enough for a safe night
at the shelter
and one 7-ounce bottle of *White Lightning.*

A good day for Mary if her parents
don't call her Marty,
talk about the son they've lost
or ask what they did wrong:
one day of relief
in her blemished mirror.

Sperm whale silenced by sonar,
polar bear
navigating melting ice,
mountain gorillas imprisoned
to keep them safe from poachers:
how do they measure their days?

So many that might have been good
tend to disappear
into the growing morass
of unquestionably bad,
no mitigating argument
against the unlucky draw.

Should we be learning to count
minutes instead of days,
or decades of global failure
as earth's temperature
rises to suck us all
into its suffocating grasp?

The Corpse Worked Hard

The old world is dying and the
new world struggles to be born;
now is the time of monsters.
—Antonio Gramsci

The corpse worked hard to be able to teach
its final lesson to full effect.
Hairless, loose skin
hanging on rachitic bone, ochre stench
and twisted limbs photographed
at Belsen, Auschwitz,
or headless in Iraq's mass graves:
memory become the image that will not fade.

The constriction of bound feet is indistinguishable
from those purple blotches
spreading across a battered woman's body,
the invisible scars on a daughter's dignity,
those special tortures
reserved for women in war,
the demands, the jokes, the justification:
locker room talk, after all.

Go back where you came from rings the same
in the ears of Mexicans, Guatemalans,
an immigrant from Syria or El Salvador,
and the child born here
afraid he will come home one day
to find his parents taken, gone:
tunnels of hope, deserts of pain,
secular rapture in this era of hate.

The swastika screams exclusion, cannot retrieve
its Sanskrit meaning, ancient symbol
of *good fortune* or *wellbeing,*
just as the man-woman symbol
on the transgender restroom
is pulled in two directions:
one inclusive, the other
planting fear in every narrow mind.

Each generation vows *never again*
as it nurtures its journey
from terror to bullied… or bully.
Crossing the line, we accumulate critical mass
as we push the tipping point past go.
Will we honor that courageous corpse
or let ourselves stagger back
into the arms of hate?

If Only

If instead of teaching his oldest son
crooked real estate
he'd shared a dream of perfect calligraphy
in the manner of sixteenth century monks.

If rather than encourage her daughter
to marry a chosen one,
leaving a string of used young women
in his wake,
she'd passed on a talent for quilting,
honest and wordless
as the surface of a mountain lake.

If the boy who grew into genocide's face
had been in first form A instead of B
and responded to the single teacher
who might have encouraged his art.

If one determined freeze refuses to release
that chunk of arctic ice
the size of New Hampshire
or the tornado slicing through Kansas
travels half a mile west
of the town it slices from your heart.

If only we could open a history book
and read about such alternative worlds
pungent and safe as gardenia trees
growing wild on plantations
of dark myth,
danger would still lurk in corners,
greed still threaten us with its deceit.

But death would be smaller,
life steadier on her feet.

When Multiple Choice
Replaced Socratic Wisdom

Future historians may dispute the moment
democracy split its seams,
too many rotten threads in the weave,
too much greed.

Some will blame money, millions or billions
for prime-time ads
launched as entertainment cum news:
fake or alternate: who knew the difference?

Others will say our elected representatives
forgot the promises they made
to us and our children and grandchildren,
busy as they were with sleight of hand.

Many will point to the moment we stopped
learning how to think for ourselves,
when multiple choice
replaced Socratic wisdom.

Few will notice it's the small things
completed our journey:
same price for a jar or carton containing less,
invented cures for invented diseases.

Our own eyes pretend they do not see
the man holding desperation's sign,
readymade narrative
laced with built in lies

like the day we accepted embedded reporters
telling our far away stories
presented as alternative fact.
We no longer know the difference.

Most won't remember a time before.
Most will wander this nation,
muted citizens as far as the eye can see,
oblivious and sorrowful

because remembering depends on
truthful words, trusted bridges
from dream to reality, thought to action,
words that say what they mean.

The Morning After

—To the children

It's the morning after and the polar bear
licks blood
from his foot's white fur.
Ice is jagged and cuts, its islands recede
to the beat of human denial.
Far to the south: a dying parrot's heart cries.

It's the morning after and beneath the wall
long scarring our southern border
tunnels carry *coyotes* and their human cargo
while real coyotes and smaller animals
burrow for daily bread, unaware
of a madman's ravings, pompous threat.

It's the morning after. I wish there was a pill.
So many hard-won battles tremble
on this map redrawn by hatred's hand.
The Bully-in-Chief stands before us:
triumphant, tricked by the deceptive weave
of his own Emperor's New Clothes.

It's the morning after and emergency rooms
fill with attempted suicides:
queer teenager, black youth, young girl
who hoped her ceiling would begin to crack,
boy whose brother was murdered by the cop
still riding his neighborhood patrol.

Six-year-old Maia tells her mother *Wake me
when Hillary wins.* The next morning
she is afraid to go to school:
If we speak Spanish in the street,
she wants to know,
will they send us away?

It's the morning after. Shock subsides
to fear and rage
throughout the world.
But beware of an elite
still measuring loss by lies and votes,
unable to hear the real stories:

It's the morning after, one of many. Listen
to the heartland's threatened factory,
another child who wakes up hungry,
love too afraid to speak its name
or the single mother of three
without a home.

Trust me rings hollow on the liar's lips.
I will fix it isn't the answer.
Only together can we resist:
by loving, creating,
and embracing the vulnerable among us
four more years.

Success

We didn't win but does that mean we lost?
For our adversary
winning is success,
seducing with content as well as form.

As our lives slow to that ponderous rhythm
where memory fills
the hidden spaces,
failure tries to imprint itself upon our flesh.

Hard to remember that winning
is about holding justice
in linked hands,
savoring its breath against tired skin,
understanding success
does not define
the essence of morality.

Super Moon

The great gold disk rides the night sky
as if trying to sweep our grief
and fear away.

They say the moon won't seem
this big again until
the year 2034.

Will we still have an earth then
that can welcome its mystery,
or will the moon

in its oblivious orbit look down
unmoved on all
we have destroyed?

Rebar

—For V.B. Price

Driving across the unsettled reaches of Chihuahua in northern Mexico, we pass through occasional towns and villages. A common sight is the great number of unfinished buildings small and large. Brick or stucco dissolve. Fingers of bent rebar reach into nothingness. I contemplate the sad sight and realize this is a scene endemic to places throughout the dependent world. A building project takes off. Then a breadwinner is fired or a child gets sick and the money runs out. Structures are left half completed: a couple of floors without a roof, the emptiness where windows or doors will never close against wind and rain.

Rebar is supposed to be invisible, the hidden support within buildings faced with more elegant materials. Its visibility speaks a language of incompletion, a half-done job.

In most parts of the world such a landscape is commonplace, expected. People live surrounded by that which is unfinished. And the unfinished weathers in place, breaks down, crumbles, eventually becomes one with the earth, only to be fashioned once more into brick or another building material and continue its cyclical job. Increased economic depression and uncertainty extend the process to the horizon and beyond.

It is its extension within—burrowing deep into minds, hearts, expectations—that compels me here. Does living in an unfinished landscape evoke, or worse promote, a sense of the unfinished life, one forever wanting, reaching, incomplete? More importantly, incapable of completion? Such a situation has political as well as psychological implications. What does it feel like to live on an unfinished landscape, an "unsettled landscape" (the title SITE Santa Fe gave the first in its Site Lines series of contemporary art biennials that explore the skewed reality in which, as Lucy Lippard so brilliantly notes, "our history emerges from the south but our nationality is tied to the north.")[1]

The poor are as inventive as the rich, and have much less with which to work. A row of coffee cans filled with bright flowers may sit on a makeshift sill beneath the glassless window of a wooden shack anywhere in Latin America. Local rocks may be arranged in designs as expressive as those set by the most sophisticated land artist. In the South African countryside, I drove past round mud houses painted bright shades of green and blue. In Peru I saw a boy who looked to be six or seven struggle up a mountain path carrying an ornamental tree on his back. Its roots were encased in earth and carefully wrapped, leaving no doubt it would be planted rather than used as firewood.

Although it isn't something to which we commonly pay attention, architecture is the art form that has the most profound impact on our lives, all our lives all the time. Think about it: depending upon our class and culture, we may read more or less, visit museums more or less frequently or not at all (familiarizing ourselves or not with painting, sculpture and other art forms), routinely listen to music or ignore its seductive beat. Dance as performance may be even farther from our everyday experience; a select

---

1. Lucy Lippard, "Invasive Species, Restlessness, Disturbances, and other Events," *Unsettled Landscapes*, Santa Fe, SITE Santa Fe, 2014, p 71.

few attend ballets or modern programs, while for most the high school prom or club date may be our last memory of engaging in dance ourselves.

Photography, only relatively recently considered an art form, lives by different rules. Its use in commercial advertising or to depict war often makes it seem trustworthy even as it lies. Assuming it as reality places us within a fictitious landscape, with all the risk and self-deception that brings. Photography's question "Is it reality or art?" is largely decided today by corporate greed and political manipulation.

Yet architecture surrounds us. It is the landscape in which we live our everyday lives: consciously or unconsciously. So much of how we see ourselves comes from where we are and what we see around us.

Without engaging in the primitivistic cliché so often associated with cave paintings now believed to be 32,000 years old, we may take note of the directness and representational freedom explicit on those cavern walls adorned with ancient bison and horses. We feel this as well when gazing at the 6,000-year-old Barrier Canyon pictographs of Utah: a profound sense of oneness between the living of life and its representation. The artists who painted such scenes on their walls surrounded themselves with a recording of their days. Contemporary murals tend to function in the same way. Commercial billboards, once outlawed on our highways by Ladybird Johnson, are crass and coercive by comparison.

A constructed architectural landscape may be chosen, but it is much more often imposed, the result of circumstances such as climate, memory, cultural accessibility, race, gender, income, mental or physical capacity, having or not having work, or being part of a family in which any of these variables is determinate.

It is winter. An Albuquerque middle school teacher asks one of her students how he slept the night before, and he looks away as he admits he spent the night "in the back yard." He quickly adds "It's okay, though, my uncle built me a shed back there." "Weren't you cold?" the teacher asks. "No," the student says, "I have an electric heater." This is normal for this child, the painful architecture of his young life.

Here in the United States, especially in the east where land is at a premium, our great cities rise, squeezing us in narrow corridors. The upward vistas speak power, literal cathedrals of corner offices we too may inhabit if we work hard, play by the rules, compete voraciously and trample those who, for whatever reason, do not make the grade. Their building materials are also synonymous with power: concrete, steel, great expanses of glass acting as mirrors in which clouds float by and other beautiful buildings are reflected.

At its wealthiest and most ostentatious, urban architecture speaks a language of tallest, biggest, best. It is not surprising that the building that eventually replaced New York's Twin Towers had to be at least as high as its predecessors. And its predecessors announced what they stood for by virtue of their soaring silhouettes. The terrorist tragedy perpetrated against the United States on September 11, 2001 was keenly felt. But at least part of what our architectural minds could come up with in memoriam was more of the same: the language of power as exemplified by size. In contrast, the quiet reflecting pool, with its etching of names, speaks more eloquently to the profundity of our loss.

At the other end of the spectrum, our cities decay. Extreme poverty is becoming endemic. In concert with economic decline, millions share space with asbestos, lead-based paint, garbage, rodents, lice. They swelter in summer, freeze in winter, drink unsafe water and scramble for welfare stamps with which to buy a minimal amount of processed food that keeps them unhealthy, prey to obesity and disease. In short, they are forced to inhabit spaces less and less fit for human life.

Identification with those spaces produces a damage impossible for one who has not experienced it to know. It is like a 24/7 extension of Native American children searching for themselves in films in which the Indians are always the outlaws, their captors the representatives of justice. Or African American, Latino and gay children watching television in which people who look like them are invariably tokens or comic relief. Except now the burden of inferiority crosses class and racial lines.

From vertical to horizontal, our suburban landscapes extend in seemingly endless vistas of residential development: miles of identical houses varied only by slight differences in color or cosmetic detail. In the 1950s we had Levittown in the east; its name synonymous with the tracts as they moved west. Today such developments blight land in Colorado, Nevada, Arizona, California—land that arguably should be protected as part of a patrimony preserved in its natural state. Overpopulation threatens water tables. Aquifers are depleted, rivers diverted, and dams create unexpected disasters. Humanity becomes part of the problem rather than the solution. And global warming makes the dilemma so much more urgent.

The tidy finished look of neat houses lining perfectly tended streets should not be confused with a well-conceived and architecturally beautiful suburban landscape. The vast senior projects around Phoenix, for example, are indicative of such insult. Distinguishable from Levittown only by their desert landscaping, melting curbs and golf-cart transport, they exude a similar dreary sameness. Most often, they are also exclusive, catering to an aging upper middle-class white clientele.

These vast housing projects feed the ever-increasing greed of developers, investors, builders and others who only care to think in the short term. But what do these projects convey to those who live in them, and to those who have come to accept them as part of the landscape? Their inhabitants undoubtedly feel fortunate to have homes. But the subliminal message is: conformity, sameness, fitting in. Don't make waves, don't challenge—mainstream ideas as well as visual panorama. Some years back, a well-known Hispanic writer in San Antonio, Texas, incurred the wrath of city fathers when she painted her house periwinkle. White and pale shades of gray were considered the only historically acceptable colors.

Erosion of the natural landscape is part of this picture. The Levittowns of the desert, with their rows of cookie-cutter houses, strip malls, and fountains that promise recirculating water, inevitably erase the wide open spaces that help us breathe, especially in the West. Our disappearing mountains and canyons. Our wildness. Our wilderness. Even our national parks, surely one of the best ideas this nation has had, have felt the squeeze in recent years. Administrations that think nothing of spending billions waging war on others' landscapes, architectures and peoples, have drastically cut back on the funding needed to preserve our untouched places.

Consider Seattle, where one can see Mount Rainier looming in all her snow-capped majesty at the end of a city thoroughfare. Imagine any western U.S. city, whose outskirts give way to deserts or high forest. Then think of the visual as well as physical congestion that emanates from unchecked building. It isn't only water overuse or increased pollution we should be worried about, but feeding or encroaching upon our sense of self. Some call this identification with nature spirituality. I call it living in place.

Our country's inner city ghettos present a different landscape (read: problem) from most in the developing world. Rather than the unfinished look of stark rebar, the image is one of boarded up homes, increasingly occupied by those who have been forced out of more livable quarters. The break didn't come while the building was still going on, but much later after life seemed secure and then suddenly didn't. Without electricity or water, a relatively recent category of people we call "homeless" take refuge in structures that have been foreclosed or abandoned. And the message here is indeed abandonment, social as well as physical. The child who cannot go to school because she has no address. The immigrant who lives nowhere.

Such slums have been claimed by urban gangs that carve them into competing turfs. Bully police patrol them, but have not yet found ways to positively connect with their communities. These neighborhoods are routine sites of illegal drug trade and drive-by shootings. Violence. Exposure. Hunger. Vulnerability. Mothers afraid to send their children to school. Children afraid to play outdoors. This is today's new urban architecture of hopelessness, a message that continues to lower the bar of the new normal.

Untended architecture isn't only exposed rebar, boarded up or unfinished buildings, overgrown yards, and pock-marked streets. Ghetto architecture includes as well the routine murders of Afro-American and Hispanic men and boys by the uniformed representatives of a system that should protect them. It is an architecture of fear, hate and terror, now indelibly engraved upon our eyes and in our cells. It is the expectation that at any moment schools, churches, theaters, malls or traffic stops may become scenes of sudden massacres. Or that police will be targets of a terrible revenge. It is the community vigil, raging and sorrowing in equal measure. It is mass resignation in the face of elected officials who overwhelmingly favor their careers over finding solutions to the wars engulfing us, and brave young people, such as those in "Black Lives Matter," who refuse to give in to that resignation.

It is a bipolar nation living on a bipolar landscape in an architecture of mixed messages.

Throughout the twentieth century, facing problems requiring new solutions countries have approached these problems in different ways. The socialist world, especially, attempted to house, feed and clothe their populations. In Cuba, where I lived from 1969 to 1980, the first years of dramatic socio-political change brought exciting innovation in all the arts. Architecture wasn't exempt. Architects—foreign as well as homegrown—designed buildings that exuded originality, innovation, beauty, use of local materials. One was Havana's National Art School. Another was an ice cream parlor with room for 1,000 at a sitting. The message was creative possibility.

Then, toward the end of that decade, the pressing problems of how to keep up with the demand for new housing, how to educate an entire nation, in short how to meet the requirements of a people in power, came up against rote "solutions" influenced by Stalinist-inspired Soviet collaboration. Rather than encourage innovation that took into account the country's tropical light, cultural history and island identity, large housing projects and schools in the countryside were built with prefabricated slabs of gray cement. This was part of a much larger assault on the arts, and the people who produced them. It has been called "The Five Gray Years."

During a public reckoning that, sadly, didn't come until 2007, the great Cuban architect Mario Coyula made a scathing critique of that period in which the opportunity to nurture a truly revolution-ary generation of Cuban architects was lost, and the country suffered a prefab landscape that negatively impacted its overall identity. There is no doubt that the readymade buildings solved immediate housing and educational needs; it took much longer to recog-nize what had been lost.

In his assessment, Coyula remembered that:

> Back then, difference wasn't seen as a revo-lutionary quality, and rigidity became a virtue rather than a defect. A provincial xenophobia rejected anything that was different or came from somewhere else. In the early seventies we had achieved architectural production of high quality, capable of taking on new projects and expanding across the country. But the dominant tendency from the end of that decade on was the use of heavy prefabricated panels produced in large factories and put in place with large cranes. Despite all evidence to the contrary, this model continued, demonstrating that mental prefabrication can be more rigid and last longer

than the technological kind [. . .]

Dogmatism in our profession also came to the School of Architecture, at that time the only one in the country. A grotesque personage arrived [at the school], and in a few short years enforced an impressive regime of absurd extremism. He pushed a technocratic approach and eliminated or mutilated all courses with cultural content. He also relegated "cultural" teachers to inhospitable places, so they would "put their feet in the earth," that is to say in the mud. His abuses were rejected by an absolute majority in an act of mass repudiation rarely seen before [. . .] It wasn't only homosexuals or people of faith who suffered. Heterosexuals, atheists and revolutionaries were also part of the collateral damage, because we became worse human beings. I was there, and I didn't raise my voice. Along with other comrades, and despite the pros and cons involved in the great social project to which we were dedicating our lives, I simply watched and kept quiet.

Like any other human project, a revolution is subject to errors, but when ethical and moral principles are violated those errors become abuses [. . .] There is the general perception that beautiful architecture must cost a lot of money, but all over the world there are good examples made of humble materials, and many horrific examples made with the most expensive [. . .] In closing, I have a question: Are we doing the sort of architecture this country deserves?[2]

---

2. Talk given by Mario Coyula (1935-2014) on March 9, 2007, at the Instituto Superior de Arte, Havana, as part of the cycle "La política cultural de la Revolución: memoria y reflexión," organized by the Centro Teórico-Cultural Criterios. http://www.criterios.es/pdf/coyulatrinquenio.pdf. Translation by MR.

This sort of deviation isn't only the product of top down control. It can arise, as well, out of moments of social disintegration. A few years ago, I was in Albania, a country about which we know far less than we do about Cuba, but one that also holds some lessons. There, too, a socialist government took its turn trying to provide a better life for people. Unlike Cuba, the experiment was mostly hidden from world view, and ended in defeat.

On one long bus ride along a makeshift road winding inland from the coast, large half-finished houses had literally been bulldozed off their foundations and stood at grotesque angles, their half-raised walls exposed to the elements. Yawning rebar was everywhere. It seemed that one big problem of the transition from socialism to a market economy was rampant corruption: someone paid someone else for a building permit and began construction, then a third person deemed the permit illegal and simply tore the home from its moorings. Perhaps a fourth or fifth person would later get rich taking bribes in exchange for a new permit. Or perhaps those involved would give up, and the landscape would retain its crazed architectural silhouette into some unknown future.

Coyula's question is one we must all ask ourselves, whoever we are and whatever landscape we inhabit: physical, cultural, artistic. We grow and develop, and pass values, perceptions and expectations on to our children and grandchildren immersed in a real surround: what we see, feel, experience. Its backdrop informs our state of mind, shapes our energy and creativity. Landscape and human-made architecture are integral to this.

Just as ingesting genetically modified or pesticide-laden foods can make us sick, just as breathing polluted air, drinking contaminated water or living near toxic waste dumps can kill us, just as absorbing a nationalist world vision can make us cruel, and living as false patriots will surely reduce us to "them and us," residing in ugly, overcrowded, blighted or unfinished architecture leads us to assume those qualities in how we think of ourselves.

Rebar or boarded up windows, out of control development or out of control police, the landscapes we live in tell us who we are. It is up to us to recognize the damage—physical, psychological, and spiritual—and put our interdisciplinary shoulders to the wheel to achieve a healthier place to live. We have the will to explore our moon, Mars, now even Venus and Pluto. Will we leave half-finished armatures as mileposts of our "progress"? Will conquest always be our language?

Pancasán

—For Víctor Rodríguez Núñez

You do for your children. That's what being a parent is about. And then, at a moment few mothers or fathers forget, one of them does for you. It might be something as small as an unprovoked smile. Or as big as a birthday gift or being helped down a flight of stairs. Unbidden, that's the thing. With some kids that moment happens at age three. With others it doesn't appear until the child, no longer a child, is thirty. And that's just the thing: if it happens at thirty, that's when he or she stops being a child.

Such is the unfolding of generations.

War turns that unfolding on its head. Impossible to wait, then, for the moment to blossom naturally, in line with a child's temperament or sense of self. Children bleed and die in wars, leaving their parents bereft. Parents bleed and die, leaving their children abandoned, furrowed by loss, often disconnected even from themselves. On Nicaragua's northern border with Honduras, in 1983, I watched a boy who looked to be four—I later found out he was seven—inch up a rocky hill, his one-legged father leaning on the small elbow lifted awkwardly to bear his lurching weight. To become his missing leg. Child as crutch. At the end of their struggle they would be home, but it would never again be the home it had been when father could be father, and child, child.

I couldn't find what had been my home, the house I had lived in almost four years, from 1980 to '84. Not yet a decade later, I was back in Nicaragua doing the fieldwork for a new book. My partner of many years had come with me, and I wanted to show her the physical scenario of so many stories, so much life and death. More challenging, I wanted to show her that tenuous place between the two, a conversation in a single voice. What that small compact little house with its front garden and Jacaranda tree had looked like in hope, in expectation, and then in war. But, once in the neighborhood, I had no idea where to turn. All the streets looked the same.

The house had been mine by several counts. I'd bought it for $5,000 from someone who obviously feared the Sandinista victory and was in a hurry to emigrate. I'd inhabited it tenderly, for more than three years making it mine with my early morning rush to work, late night exhaustion, gatherings of comrades, laughter, Joan Baez and Holly Near on an old turntable, the scent of furtive kisses and pungency of black beans.

Two of my daughters, Ana and Ximena, came with me from Cuba to live in recently liberated Nicaragua. They did their homework on that house's thick round dining room table, conspired with friends behind the door of the small bedroom they shared, stood tall against its jamb so I could mark another year's growth, added the sounds of their voices to the music written in its brick and mortar.

Like so many young girls their age, they lied to me about the men—not boys—they were dating. And in that time and place they also went out to pick coffee and do their parts in a ragtag people's militia. Looking back, our family life in Pancasán (the neighborhood named after the Sandinista's first armed battle, not that many years before) returns in flashes of extraordinary drama. Yet now, try as I will, I can't find the house.

Almost from the moment of my initial arrival, Managua had shown me its death mask. The war against Somoza was freshly over, and hundreds of fallen comrades lay loosely covered in shallow earth along highways and in fields and backyards. Along with many others, I covered my nose and mouth with a damp handkerchief against the stench of decayed flesh, put shoulder to shovel and helped dig up their bones, fragments of bloodied clothing, a few pages of poetry, a scrap of paper bearing what's left of a phrase washed by seasons of tropical rain, a skull that comes loose from the rest of its skeleton in my astonished hands. No one who has done this can forget the impregnating odor of dead humans; its nauseating intensity can be recalled years later, overpowering every living cell. Once removed from their temporary resting places, we would move those earlier dead to burial in cemeteries, where family and friends could erect proper stones, bring flowers, mourn their loss. Much too soon we would prepare for fresher dead, the next round in war's unending cycle.

I remembered a night at the house I cannot find, when a good neighbor came to our rescue, revolver drawn. I too slept with a sidearm atop my little bedtable, and hearing someone jump the garden wall had prompted me to shout for that neighbor's help. We were constantly attentive to incursions of one sort or another. Those were tumultuous years, in which the Contras, paid for and encouraged by my government, had begun to threaten the capital. That particular night resolved itself peacefully. Whoever had entered our garden was nowhere to be found. Would the next invasion end so peaceably?

Along the main highway to Masaya: La Margarita. An eatery serving chicken tacos with a sprinkling of fresh cheese and tall glasses of tropical fruit shakes. I remember the stout pale green body of the old Osterizer used to blend those shakes. My friend Pat Hynds and I would meet there once a week—was it Tuesday or Wednesday?—for lunch and to debrief and encourage each other as the danger surrounding us closed in. I worked farther out along that same highway, my office in one of a series of large upper-class mansions abandoned by their owners when the Revolution took power. Circular bands, circumscribed by class, floated behind my eyes: ribbons of different hues marking the level each ring occupied around the capital. The farther out, the higher the class. Until you reached real countryside with its rural poor. Down by the lake squalor reeked. Like successive layers of a birthday cake that remain only partially consumed in memory.

I found La Margarita—it was called something else now—crossed the highway and entered the old neighborhood. None of the streets had names. Addresses were typically: "From the big tree, two blocks in the direction of the lake, a hundred yards up." Or: "Two yards past Señor García's house and a block to the north." The big tree might have been uprooted a generation back, Señor García moved who knew when or where. Natives retained a knowledge of place that didn't depend upon such detail. No neat grid here. Just seemingly endless curved strips of houses that looked alike. None of them looked like mine. I gave up. I wanted to take my woman there, but didn't know which way to turn. Familiarity soured on my tongue.

Then you, Víctor, told me you would take us. You knew the house, you said, and its current occupants. My breath quickened, temperature rose. Someone came to the door, smiling. Behind him I could see the round wooden table, the set of four carved rocking chairs, and those ugly green plastic oversized cushions inviting rest but reluctant to release a body that had the audacity to plop itself down on one. Some of my framed photographs were still on the walls, but the darkroom was no longer in use. My eyes strained to glimpse what was beyond a half open bedroom door

"Do you want to see the backyard?" he interrupted my reverie. "I think that's where you lived. Am I right?"

I didn't want him to be right, his memories of my life here sharper than my own. Suddenly I didn't want to retrieve those nights sleeping with one hand on the grip of the revolver I'd gotten from a guy named Manuel at one of the big city markets. A revolver I'd never used and hoped I'd never have to. Nights and nights when sleep refused to come. Only tears, spilling from eyes that wouldn't close. A priest friend finally took to sleeping on the floor beside my bed so I could gain uneasy rest.

But of course I did want those nights. And the days between. Every one of them.

I was back on early morning patrol now, once a month, walking through streets in shadow, past houses like my own. No one out there but whomever was scheduled for that particular slot. I remembered patrolling with a friend from Ecuador, who had come to Nicaragua to join the fight against Somoza but arrived too late. The war was over, or so we thought. This had to make do as his contribution. One night he didn't show up until an hour past our assigned time. I complained and he only laughed at what he called my gringa penchant for being on time. What could it matter, he scoffed.

Friday night dinners at the Jesuit House is one of the memories I cherish, one that never leaves. Five of those renegade fathers lived together, opening their home to communal meals once a week, offering comfort even to a non-believer like me. Years later two of them were murdered in Guatemala. A few months ago a third died at the end of a long life: one of those who gave his years and all his intelligence to our broken dream. It occurs to me—inveterate atheist—that Nicaragua was a plateau where we all rested for a while. Rested and once again tried to make something new. Although it never felt like rest.

Like the house I couldn't find, the Revolution we made and tried to grow dissipated like a balance bar in shambles. The United States waged its always-ready covert and overt war upon our hope. Too many of the Sandinistas themselves went bad, allowing greed and corruption in where singular sacrifice once stood. Deviance corroded justice. Those few who carry revolution's ideals today are no match for the takeover of entrenched power—hiding behind the same words but smelling of deceit. The words that told us who we were back then now wear costumes of betrayal.

I wonder if losing the internal map that would have taken me easily to my old home means I have also lost pieces of myself from those four years: the house and its anticipation of a different future, hours in the darkroom or those spent on the shadow streets of nighttime patrol?

Is that place called the Sandinista Revolution still there, somewhere, like the home I once inhabited or the roadside eatery before it changed its name?

Where does place live in the ether that surrounds us?

When the memories fade, where do the shattered pieces fall?

Wild Patience

A wild patience has taken me this far.
—Adrienne Rich

I am reaching the edges
of my body,
touch fjords
glowing beneath northern lights
or graceful as the royal palm
and fecund as the lichen-covered glyphs
in Mayan lowlands.

Gently I place a fingertip
against skin
softened by years
of risk and setting sun.
Peering in any mirror
I note sudden protrusions,
unwelcome overlay.

The consults come more often now,
catch threat before it explodes,
each reassurance a whole new calendar.

My body's edges beckon conspiratorially,
inviting memory, gratitude,
wild patience and peaceful countdown.

Where Silence Lives

Inside the silence of possibility
words quiver and stretch,
each gathering breath
for that moment
when its time will come.

Between one word and another
silence gains momentum
badgering those words to change sides,
daring them to try and force it
to draw its last breath.

The parenthesis of privilege grows
where silence grins,
greeting us with open arms,
singing louder
and always on key.

This is not the silence of ancient life
become memory stone
through the loneliness of time,
not landscape
embracing us.

Remember the good Cistercian monk
writing fire from silence,
urging us to listen and speak,
the palms of his hands
creased in doubt.

Remember the woman silenced
by a slap across her mouth
who may hide or rise,
stockpiling her words
for a future that will not come.

The child's silence only pleases
those who traffic in shame,
live by stupefying ritual
and cannot remember
where they've been.

We age and silence becomes time,
stretches toward a rim
of horizon
we hope will welcome us
in a language we understand.

Meanwhile, poets always choose
to risk surprise,
take silence by both shoulders,
shake hard and wait
for whatever drops from the tree.

Conversation

Passengers are still boarding.
you settle in your seat
and the conversation starts
one row back.
He asks her if she lives
in Minneapolis, or is headed home.

She mentions a wedding, not hers,
and he remembers
the last out of town wedding
he attended, chuckles
in a way that says
there's more to the story.

They move on to weather,
a restaurant he knows,
even cancer and suicide: intimacy
quickly reorganizing itself
when neither will see the other
again. Or will they?

Through the hum of the plane's
tired engine revving up
and the chatter of 150 other voices,
theirs, though unseen,
clearly win by decibel and need:
part inflection, part longing.

Two hours later you have
the basics of both lives:
his war service, family situation,

advice. Her best friend's dilemma
and how she tries to help
but isn't appreciated.

Strangers confiding everything even as
the important conversations
remain impossible:
when and how to die,
stop wars, tell parents
I am living in the wrong body.

Older to younger, race to race,
boss to worker
or worker to boss.
Lovers in any configuration
and the national conversation
that might save us all.

I have never ever worn anything pink,

preferring black, or an exuberant explosion
of rainbow colors. I cover my breast
with the multi-threaded story
Guatemalan women's blouses tell.

I have never toppled or battered my strong feet
in five-inch heels, go barefoot where I can.
A long time since I've forced my flesh into elastic prisons
or covered my truth-telling lips in red.

My scent is soap, my hair's hue thin white of age.
I remember my son's nine-year-old eyes
recoiling before the makeover
masking the eyes he loved

when a friend, who assumed we'd thrill
to cosmetic correction, labored hours
to erase my flaws and surprise him
with the grotesque mask.

That memory continues to speak to me
of what the fashion bullies call flaws
creating shame so they may profit
from its deception.

Today I take refuge in those so-called flaws: maps
revealing a life lived,
and would expose the industry that sells submission,
usurping beauty's name.

Products

This one does miracles, that one
keeps you looking ten years
younger—any ten years.
Hair luxuriant and full,
unblemished skin,
age-spots erased:
all you have to do is take one look
at Jennifer Aniston's digitally perfect face.

Oils and creams boast they are plants,
words like *natural* and *organic*
excite the senses.
Vitamins guarantee
abundant energy
and there's a one-pill fix
for everything from reptile dysfunction
to growing up.

It's the product you need, must have,
cannot live without
unless the nearest makeup counter
is too far from your tent city
or there is no aloe vera
growing along the trail of tears
that crosses the border
where you left your heart.

Nothing at All to Learn

Original manuscript pages written
by the first woman to fly
or the idol who reveals affairs
we've known about for years
top Sotheby's sales this season:
readers eager for words
written with them in mind.

These are not broken wings
folded across breasts
that sorrow or burn
but maps inviting judgment
of those not yet here
who will wonder
at what we thought and did.

I too keep a journal I share
with family and friends.
I too write for posterity
—as the saying goes—
eager to leave an open window
on this life I inhabit,
what I see and feel and know.

But today I remember the diary
I kept as a teenager
traveling with my parents
to places they thought exotic:
The waiter's nails were clean,
I wrote after lunch in Rio:
young arrogance, sad legacy.

Sometimes the words that say the most
are those we would erase
from every memory,
disown from assumed superiority
where we pretend
we were born in perfect balance,
nothing at all to learn.

Marking Time

—For my great grandson,
Guillermo Alvarez Randall

The moment comes and goes
and I've written another book.
In every minute her love explodes:
cascading sun-streaked touch
through memory's certainty.

Is it only age condensing time,
squeezing its sides in laughter,
keeping it safe along the trail
hugging the tallest mountain?
Is the enemy's word always complicit?

My children feel their way, grandchildren explore
or reject those paths stained by my blood.
Time looks me in the eye
and I weep because we will not witness
our great grandchildren marking their rhythms.

The poem takes its place in time, steps back,
then surveys its accidental map
and flies.
My days grow shorter,
each word deep blue, in waiting.

Our Round Heads

Our thoughts like tiny dragonflies
buzz in our round heads
where technology's latest scans
reveal only synapses
flashing from emitter to receptor.

Their fluttering wings mimic the sound
of a million migrants walking,
a billion dying children,
this language of denial
that cannot survive translation.

What we know in our round heads
are limitless rooms,
unfenced spaces
where our thoughts may procreate
before they change direction.

Late Works

Late works constitute a form of exile.
—Edward Said

How to speak and be heard
shapes our mirror image
from birth or before.

As we cross each border
our need swells,
temperature rises.

How to speak and be heard
in this new place,
arriving with off-rhythm heart

beating in remembered step,
those who greet us
turning away?

I write this lifetimes past
your bedtime,
from an unmapped territory

where all my mirrors
are cracked,
the itch has turned to pain

and nothing matters so much as
remembering, speaking,
passing it on

before new tendrils on strong vines
pull my tired cells
to earth.

I Like Being Old

I really do like being old, having come this far,
having heard and seen, mistaken and known
and done. Especially done.

You may think it resignation, making the best
of the inevitable bad deal,
a joke perhaps.

But what could be better than these fertile memories,
moments the greatest novelist couldn't make up,
people and places shaping a century?

Great grandchild moving beyond grandchildren
who take my children's lives high
and extend my own?

Experience enough to separate what matters
from what isn't worth one moment
of concern?

True, I must pay attention to stiff joints
and creaking bones, navigate each step
up or down a flight of stairs:

challenge against the fateful fall,
wonder about a wavering kidney,
eat less of what I love

and more of that cafeteria-bland food
I saw my parents repeat
day after boring day.

No longer can I toss a full head of hair
but carefully comb what remains
to cover blotches of pale scalp,

wonder why so little grows
where it once did me proud,
so much where it isn't welcome.

My body moves more slowly now
while my mind, when present,
is an ocean of furious waves

sinking ships and revealing
underwater marvels
simultaneously.

Wisdom travels arthritic fingertips,
memory prunes itself
of bitter twigs

as it grows roots that ask questions
and will help sustain
generations beyond my touch.

It's all good. More than good as I embrace
this red rock landscape, this place
that belongs to me

and absorb each whispering sound
of language and wind,
with you, love: brilliant pollinated center

of our extraordinary many-petaled life.

Asking Why Why Why

Slamming that fresh-faced couple
invading my office
Sandinista Culture Ministry 1981
as if they owned a land
that had never drunk their blood.

Asking why why why
of the big man
whose word was law,
then refusing to take my eyes from his,
crossing demure off the list.

Getting off the F Train two stops
before mine
because the temperature rising
between my breasts
told me it's time, right now or never.

Reading the perfect poem I wanted
to believe had been written to me
although I knew it wasn't,
its words like veins
mapping the flesh beneath my skin.

Moments that part my shoulder blades
challenge my eighty years
as I ask when I will see around a corner
the road glancing off
toward change that trembles and waits.

Not my children's births
or the major battle won
or when you showed up,
a single rose in your gym bag
meant for me.

Not the moments that changed me
but those others that only bent
direction a fraction of a degree.
Not the gulp of precious air
but subtlest breeze:

unhurried, syllables
I have always understood.

I Love Birds

Please don't text me.
I have
arthritis in my fingers
making it painful to respond.

And while offering such evidence of age
let me ask you
don't embed an emoticon
in your mails.

I prefer your unique expression
to the little yellow faces
with their identical smiles
or frowns.

Also, the idea of embedding
brings thoughts
of embedded reporters,
—an oxymoron—
sold narratives and loyalty
to those who do not wish us well.

Don't communicate with me
via Facebook.
I don't trust
its security measures.
Who is secure today?

You will not be able to tweet me,
I've kept my distance
from that modality,
don't care what non-thought
you're having at the moment.

Yet I love birds, especially the Road Runner
sitting quietly on our fence,
only occasionally greeting me
in her language of clicks.

I Come from a Long Line of Women

I come from a long line of women
who compulsively counted to ten
or touched both sides of a doorframe
before entering or leaving a room.

I do not know if the men in my family
had these psychological tics
or what other small acts sustained them
through the years.

Acts such as taking what wasn't theirs
and making us promise not to tell,
building walls of secrets
around their privilege.

If they did have visible tics, they kept them
hidden: men neither confess
nor engage in odd behavior, at least
not where others can see.

Among the women, no one talked about
her own suspect quirks
although many told tales of others
as if they themselves were innocent.

Despite my best intention, I still dry every drop
of water glistening on faucet chrome,
do routine tasks in necessary order,
count before answering phone or door.

At eighty, I freely admit to these acts,
their power to keep me calm,
their harmless gifts of comfort
in a dangerous world.

Suggestion of White on Black

Eight-by-ten images tumble forward
sounding against a granite floor.
Each is inverted, suggestion
of crisp white lines on a black surface:
more placard than negative.

These are the beloved poets: Gelman
and Diane, Roque and Susan,
some gone, others still journeying
and all having to prove their left-bank
allegiance by temperature and grit.

I keep asking: Is it Gaza's West Bank
you are talking about or Paris
in the 1930s? Perpetual danger
or safe-haven in the curve of a nose,
arch of an eyebrow, clench of a jaw?

Even Paris in the thirties was struggling
against war's menacing shadow.
Even tolerance and creativity
proved vulnerable
to the acrid smell of hate.

Dreams have a way of reordering
a face's remembered features,
poking me with questions,
demanding choices irrelevant
and unacceptable in wakeful time.

Meanwhile the gestural portraits fall,
the din they make
cacophonous in my ears.
Must I translate language
I can neither excuse nor justify?

Marjorie

*Traumatic events are extraordinary, not because they occur
rarely, but rather because they overwhelm the ordinary
human adaptations to life... They confront human
beings with the extremities of helplessness and terror,
and evoke the responses of catastrophe.*
—Judith Lewis Herman

In my family, her name wasn't mentioned
without that knowing look,
raised eyebrow implying
there was a whole lot of backstory,
none of it good.

Nymphomaniac was the word they used,
said she would go with anyone:
cabdriver, doorman, someone she ran into
on the street: black, brown, young, old.
Imagined images flared.

They put her away for her own good
they said, and I knew they meant
institutionalized, not for her benefit
but to keep the family unsullied by scandal,
free from embarrassing questions.

Marjorie was curious. I remember a letter
carefully penned on embossed paper
—dark blue on light—childish writing
asking about my life in Cuba:
We don't learn much about that country here.

Was she locked up then, or did she write
that letter between hospital stays?

And where was home?
Who did what
to Marjorie's childhood?

What terrible secret was she trying to purge
from her flesh in each sad encounter?
Who truly deserved to be locked away
in that time before the secrets
rebelled and spoke?

Called Devotion by Some,
Prostitution by Others

When 92-year-old Sashimani Devi died, the last
of Lord Jagannath's living wives was gone.
Married to a wooden image
much like Catholic sisters wed
the martyred Christian savior,
Sashimani entered the temple age seven,
one of 25 unmarried girls who grew

into womanhood dancing, bathing
and rubbing lotion
into the polished skin of her husband god,
performing intimate songs and dances
to lull him to sleep, offering her life
to a fate called devotion by some,
prostitution by others.

By the 1990s, when temple authorities tried
to recruit a new generation of ritual dancers
there were no volunteers.
But Sashimani remained proud
of her status. *He is my husband
and I his wife* she explained as she fulfilled
a tradition 5,000 years old.

Before that last ritual dancer exited this world
a scholar brought Sashimani to public view,
had her perform once more
after years of lonely retirement.
I thought of Korea's Comfort Women
serving Japanese soldiers, World War II,
or Geishas whose work is deemed art

and young Thai girls sold into sexual slavery:
international network or common pimp,
contract of intellect or flesh.
I think of every high school
homecoming queen or cheerleader,
every housewife for whom
Victoria's Secret offers a glimmer of possibility.

Had We Known

Your parents threatened brimstone
and Rapture,
strung you up in their murder cult,
survivalist religion / survival as religion
leaving you split with pain
you still resist
day after agonizing day.

Your father's Alpha stance and Jesus,
mother trembling on shaky ground.
Until brother came along, you were
the boy-girl they sent to charm school
hoping to reap conformity,
your conscious, kind, ferocious artist's spirit
threatening their secrets.

Even in my family, where love tried hard,
cycles of hurt remain unbroken,
old chains sound, their weight
heavy on tender skin.
One lie birthing another
until all surfaces
sprout their lichen of denial.

My parents' first surviving child, I
was supposed to be everything:
beautiful, smart,
while presenting
an acceptable image,
living to their expectations,
bringing no shame.

The woman Mother wanted but feared to be,
protecting her need
but never privy to her secrets.
Almost boy, but girl enough
to brag about with friends,
applauded for courage
except in the struggles of my choice.

You remember the mortuary basement
of a renegade church,
peel away one layer of always
only to find another
cowering beneath its claw-shaped fingers.
Release and entrapment vying for places
at your table even now.

I remember my peach-colored blanket
doing battle with
those orange ears of poison
growing on our garden fence.
Grandfather's eyes
menacing behind the attic door
hidden in my bedroom closet.

I think of my own children,
and theirs,
each suffering the roles
we would never have assigned them
had we known.

Comparing Notes

Was I waiting somewhere
quiet or eager
when your first Margaret
failed to survive.

Nine months later I came along
and once again
you chose Margaret
as your firstborn's name.

I always wondered about
your insistence
or lack of imagination
as if there were no other names.

I'd ask and you'd say you felt
you'd been pregnant
eighteen months.
Or you'd avoid the question.

Until a year or so before you died
we switched places—
the challenge in your court now.
I don't know where you come up

with such things, you have
the wildest imagination.
Mother/daughter
tug of war.

Sometimes on sizzling summer days
temperature rising
in my throat
I think of my older sister Margaret,

if we compared notes I'd have
a life of unfair advantage:
all the answers on my side,
all the questions on hers.

Communal Property

A small chair runs the risk of being considered cute. I'm talking about a child sized chair, not simply a lightweight version of an ordinary piece of furniture. There are chairs made specifically for children to sit in, and others that seem more decorative, like oversize toys. Little Mexican chairs with woven straw seats and brightly painted birds and flowers on their two wooden back slats rise in memory. We used to see them lined up along the highway around Oaxaca—glimpses of color pleading with us to stop. And then at four times the price in elegant crafts shops along Avenida Reforma. The antique malls of New England invariably sell one or more of a more sedate version, small replicas displaying the skill of master carpenters going back to pioneer times.

The lead character in this story is a graceful little rocker that lived in the apartment given to us by Cuba's revolutionary government when we landed in Havana mid-1969. Like so many others displaced by lost wars or saved following harrowing escapes, we had taken refuge in that First Free Territory of America. First and sadly, as it turned out, only.

Cuba received us, making good—family by family or orphaned child by orphaned child—on its promise of internationalist solidarity. Revolutionaries from all over Latin America and the rest of what we then called the Third World showed up: desperate, sometimes badly wounded or bewilderingly displaced.

The bourgeois families of island aristocracy had been fleeing for a decade by then, chased out by their own fears of the "phantom stalking a continent," in this case a tropical Caribbean island. They left behind crumbling mansions filled with the trappings of their class and taste.

Those mansions became schools, clinics, cultural centers. Along Miramar's once-elegant Fifth Avenue, at five each afternoon thousands of multicolored students ran laughing and shouting from those houses designated as classrooms, toward dinner in yet others revamped as dining halls. Occasionally those students tapped the walls of their newly converted dormitories and discovered hidden treasures, possessions those leaving expected to retrieve when Fidel was defeated and they'd get their country back. They believed this would happen rather sooner than later. Objects left in plain sight were taken to a large warehouse where Aida Santamaría—fairy godmother of regal bearing and unusual beauty—designated them to furnish the homes and apartments given to people like ourselves, who came seeking safety or simply wanting to put our shoulders to the creaking wheel of mid twentieth century social change.

The little rocker was made of well-turned wood, graceful and sturdy. Had it been a favorite of some child now growing up in Miami or New Jersey? Did a young girl miss its smooth feel, gentle motion? It appeared in place, as if it had always been there, along with a worn living room couch with two matching armchairs, recently reupholstered but newly torn again. A sturdy dining room table. Beds whose mattresses had long since relinquished firmness or comfort. And a dressing table at which I would write a dozen books

The Louis the XIV-style dressing-table-turned-desk had once been covered in sectional gilt-edged mirrors: facing for its drawers and now-cracked top. Some of those mirror-faced slabs were broken, others missing entirely, revealing the unfinished wood beneath. It stood just a bit high for writing but, as I say, saw completion of many books, all written between eleven at night and three in the morning, many with a diaper pail sitting upon its left front corner, stench of urine and ammonia invading the air.

Our apartment was on the ninth floor, with a terrace looking diagonally toward the sea. This terrace was enclosed by windows, some panes of glass broken or missing and their handles, meant to swivel them in and out, clogged with the briny buildup that had long since kept them at half-mast: neither capable of being fully extended nor safely shut against the gale force winds that assaulted Havana's coast with seasonal regularity. Because of the United States' ferocious economic blockade, by the end of the Revolution's first decade building and repair materials were unobtainable, distant memories. All that needed repair or refurbishment stood waiting, as if in perpetual stasis.

We gratefully received the selection of furnishings picked out for us. If no longer elegant, or in some cases particularly functional, they were certainly more than adequate to the needs of our family of six. As we made friends, and visited their homes, we began to realize how privileged we were.

The little rocking chair seemed an anomaly, a last-minute offering added to the lot by some functionary who may have thought: *Who knows where this family comes from or what it's been through, but surely there must be children for it to have been assigned an apartment with three bedrooms and two baths. Perhaps the little chair will become a child's favorite, and be cherished again.*

I will digress here and speak for a moment about Cuban rocking chairs. They are ubiquitous across the island, often arranged in long rows or grouped in sets of four, gracing parlors and verandas from ostentatious great houses to one-room bohios. They might be richly carved oak or mahogany, or crude pine. Did they arrive with fifteenth century Spanish immigration, or were they fashioned by Africans surviving the Middle Passage? Are they reminiscent of the influx of immigrants from nearby Haiti, who had come to work in the cane fields of the east? They seemed to have nothing at all to do with the United States, Cuba's northern neighbor that had exerted its influence in so many other ways.

Funeral homes knew those rocking chairs intimately; I never attended a Cuban wake that didn't have its long double row, in which grieving family and friends rocked slowly, fanning themselves through long nights of suffocating sorrow. Broken but still serviceable versions could be seen on porches in any city neighborhood. In the most remote reaches of countryside, a lone rocker might be the star piece of furniture, inevitably offered a guest. In the Miami airport gate area from which I have departed to Cuba in more recent years, the presence of such chairs made me feel as if I had already arrived.

Our little rocker was a perfect miniature of those full-sized versions, its back and arms elegantly proportional. But it didn't turn out to be a family favorite. Not at least insofar as its use. We cleaned house periodically, moving it here and there among its larger siblings. Our youngest, Ana, the only one who would have fit its seat, never sat in it that I recall. No one took it to his or her room, claiming it as theirs. To me it spoke of adornment rather than necessity. Perhaps that's what attracted me. It became unique, a stand-in for the years of art, chosen dinnerware, and other treasures we'd been forced to leave behind when we fled Mexico and Cuba took us in.

Yes, to me the little rocker was precious. Which is why—forty years later—I am still at a loss to explain why I destroyed it in a fit of uncontrolled rage. Is it really true that we tend to destroy what we love best?

The story goes like this. It must have been sometime in 1975 or '76. Ana's father Robert and I were coming to the explosive end of our seven-year union. We had gotten together in Mexico, during the 1968 student rebellion. I had moved naturally into that movement, product of a decade of living and working in the country, experiencing its great freedoms and devious repressions, participating in its citizen response.

Robert, nine years younger, had recently arrived on his own personal revolutionary quest, his version of what drew so many young people from a North then raging from Greenwich Village to Vietnam. He was adventurous but also committed. He seemed loyal. We'd fallen in love and begun to live together shortly before I was forced underground. Our daughter, Ana, was three months old when, fearing for their lives, we opted to send her and her brother and sisters on to Cuba before us.

Now, several years into our life in Havana, the relationship was falling apart. Everything was taking a toll: my feminism and the gender struggles of those years, smash monogamy vs. male exceptionalism, divergent interpretations of what life in revolution meant and what this Revolution expected of each of us, our age difference and who can say what else?

What we still had in common was we loved our children.

Physical separation was difficult, still is in a country in which housing is at a premium and separated or divorced couples continue to share the same space, often for years. Our U.S. middle-class white privilege turned grace under fire on its head.

Robert, always more intellectually facile than I, quoted Wittgenstein. Each of us accumulated the requisite number of anxious pleadings: *I didn't mean what I said last night.* Or *You know I love you.* Finally, I had nowhere to go but deep into my woman's rage.

The little rocking chair happened to be in my line of sight. I picked it up and hurled it at Robert, who easily stepped aside. It crashed across the room, cleaving one rocker from its frame and splintering the other; then lay, defenseless and broken on the granite floor. I was instantly as shocked as my inquisitor, who turned to me and said: *You realize you are destroying state property.* Or maybe he said: *You realize you are destroying communal property,* reminding me that what had been given us to use was not ours to break. The expression, although true, was a cliché. It would have been more insightful for him to say my conduct, in front of our young children, was totally inappropriate. It would have been insightful for me to have understood that on my own.

I remember his response as typical of other phrases of his during those years, phrases that would undoubtedly shame him today just as much of my own youthful verbiage surfaces embarrassing and trite in retrospect. Our dialogue started and stopped like a train on a broken track. Robert moved out, and in with a generous friend; the children and I remained in the apartment, for which I continued to pay ten percent of Robert's salary as rent—because even in socialist revolution the man's job was considered more relevant than the woman's.

A few years later a new partner, Antonio, fixed the rocker with braces of abandoned wood, found nails hammered straight so they could serve once more, and a homemade glue the ingredients of which I no longer remember. Antonio fixed things. From an impoverished Colombian family that had been part of the great 1940s migration to Venezuela, where it settled in a shantytown above Caracas, his class origin had taught him the real value of communal property. For him, none of it was rhetorical. He too had come to Cuba from the front lines of liberation struggle. He too felt a deep loyalty to the Revolution's generosity, and protective of its loaners.

The little chair, with its serviceable but awkward fix, had lost its charm. It had also become a permanent accusation, staring at me day in and day out, reminding me always that misplaced rage serves no productive end. Perhaps its constant presence helped me grow.

The Ring

—For Lynne DeSilva-Johnson

In retrospect, I might have noticed a change the day before. Uneasy tingling in my joints, especially elbows and knees. Arthritis? Not really that painful. In diminishing flashes, I remember going to sleep thinking about aging, wondering where the next modest ache would mock the body that still served me so well.

It isn't until I wake the next morning, stretch myself the length of my bed and raise myself on one elbow, that I know something is jarringly wrong. Pieces that do not fit. Unnerving, then frightening. Not quite memories, the rhythmic tingling conforms a knowledge that seems always to have been in me, freeing from the entanglement of time. What we take for granted, as they say.

The bed itself is narrower than when I settled into sleep. Narrower and also different. I turn to where my love's body always meets me, warm and smelling faintly of hypoallergenic skin cream. I touch air. I'm almost always awake before she is and take care not to rouse her as I slip from my side of the bed. But now I am alone, lower to the ground, and the sheets feel unfamiliar. In fact, they aren't sheets as I know them, but rough fabric smelling of desert wind and horses. My body, when I manage to pull my senses back into it, is one I cannot recognize—either by external touch or from within.

Thin. Small. Spindly arms and legs. Youthful, and then discovery descends upon me like rain: I am a child, but with rapidly fleeing sensations of another body, another self. As this realization breaks through, I fight to hold onto a corner here, a disappearing sliver of shadow there. Edges of body knowledge curl into my secret places, burrowing out of mind, sight, sense.

Voices. At first they come from an unknown lexicon, strange guttural tones I strain to decipher. Gradually I understand: a man asking for his break-fast, a woman answering in gentle coaxing tones but with a dynamic I can't unlock. Like putting a knife to an orange, beginning to separate a circular strip and suddenly the whole outer skin falls away. The language is in me but the words hold silhouettes of other words, weaving under and through them-selves, crossing out and writing above and below the line, glyphs hiding within glyphs, gaining definitive shape against this soft morning light. As I mouth each, its predecessor fades. Out of reach. Gone. A known world beyond my touch, disappearing with the sounds that speak for it.

Another world taking its place.

Each departing word leaves a piercing sadness, raw in my throat, beginning to close in terror. Where am I? Who am I? What is this place, and why is it becoming more familiar as dawn unfolds about me? I am like the pollen of a large flower, its powder lifting on air then floating back down to settle in random pattern.

Yet random is the single word I would not use to describe my plight.

Now I am jolted back to the body sitting at the edge of a pile of shaggy blankets piled between the small bed and a doorway of hanging beads. No door, only meager partition. It is from a still-obscure adjoining room that the increasingly familiar voices approach.

I stare at myself. Natural light, still thin, reveals matchstick arms hanging from hunched shoulders. I am dressed, but shiver. My hair is no longer scant and white, struggling to cover expanses of puffed pink flesh—a fading of memory—but coarse and long and black. I pull its strands to cheeks and scrawny neck, then run my fingers through its heft. Horse-blanket straw. The memory of an old woman's deceptive salon-cut disappears.

A pale circle on my left hand's ring finger begs to be touched; but when I explore the absence of what is no longer there, loss rises anguished in my throat. Right thumb and forefinger search in vain, grow frightened and cold. A bitter taste overtakes me. And the bitterness streams through pools, excess saliva my tongue tries frantically to swallow back down my throat. An unknown replaces what seconds before seemed dependable but strangely illusive: the temperature of a beloved body, a scent so familiar it might be my own.

The woman whose caressing tone I've begun to understand appears at the opening between this alcove and the chamber beyond, the one from where the voices come. She smells of olive oil and dirty kerosene. She holds a weight of ordinary days. She is speaking to me. Her words form pictures, gradually vertical in their clarity. She wants me to get up, fetch water. From where? How to perform a task I cannot yet decipher?

Begin again.

Begin again.

These two words remain unspoken but scrawled in heavy black script, a palpable remonstration. As the woman's phrases enter me, I turn them over, grasp meaning here, something almost remembered. What needn't be imagined to be done. She smiles.

I smile back, not quite so afraid. My dry lips part, then close and separate again. In my cheek a fragile muscle twitches. I reach up with trembling fingers to press it into stillness. I want to pull sounds from my throat, tongue, teeth, lips that may bridge this invisible border.

Taste rises again, the rancid taste of fear. My slim body heaves, as if to give up what it has been forced to swallow. Then it settles. Time sputters in my hands like a campfire going out. Its particles float to my eyes, anticipating questions before they form. With childlike certainty, I know each new understanding obliterates some fragment of a place before, perhaps erasing it forever. I try to hold on, but a dark wind threatens. The naked ring finger feels hobbled, taken by a force I cannot decipher. I am torn between a need to know who and where I am and a cloud of nostalgia already blanching into porous sands.

Sands. Yes, although this is a small apartment building in a neighborhood of others, although I sense many like it crowding in on all sides, this is a place of sand. Through an open window, other windows, other buildings, still-garbled street sounds. I glimpse morning light turning old stone and modern steel to flaming orange. The names of colors are comforting. They anchor me. I hold a brief memory of watermelon mountains glowing briefly just before dusk, then they are gone. A thousand shades of brown. Cobalt sky as big as the one that rises here, but sheltering a different life. Gray greens that hold a faint scent of water swollen in their withered arms.

Gone.

All gone.

The woman is telling me to go to a courtyard and bring water from an earthen jar almost as tall as I am. I follow my body. It tells me where to find the wooden stool, where the dipper hangs, how to lean into the jar's coolness and lift the water out, spilling it carefully into a basin at my feet. My body knows not a drop of precious liquid must be wasted. This is a dry place.

Dry doesn't frighten me. It feels familiar and comfortable, if also thin and precarious. But something hangs ominous beyond my immediate line of sight. The dull drone of city sounds bore into my inner ear: danger writ large. The torn strip of a vaguely remembered other place separates me from a terror I try to expel from consciousness.

Carefully replacing the large jar's cover, I carry the basin to where Mother flips fragrant rounds of bread on a hot surface. Now I know she is Mother, and the man, whose words are clear as the surface of an ancient pool of water, Father. He inclines his head, motioning me to sit beside him on the floor. Breathing in the command of his gesture, I continue to stumble on shards of fear, as if each movement toward obedience carries me along a path from which there can be no return.

There is no choice, and I sit beside the man who looks like me—ominously? comfortingly? I take the flat bread he offers, touch it to my lips. Still, my eyes travel, searching my surroundings, turning corners inside out. The surface of this place is sewn shut, its seams invisible and indivisible, not a loose thread anywhere. Yet I know I have come from somewhere else. If only I could find the door, a loose end of the weave, hold on tight, follow it out.

Follow the colors or numbers: two paths and I don't know if either leads to the place I want, need, can sometimes remember.

Home? What role does direction play in this game that is no game.

I do know this breakfast is different, special. A prologue to something.

Hello?

Goodbye?

Hello?

Time rubs up against my small body and a faint wave of nausea carries me once more into momentary dizziness. Memories of another time spar with memories of another place, another knowledge, another language and personhood. Briefly I balance atop one swaying tray of a giant scale, swinging dizzyingly from a height hidden in clouds beyond my sight. A web of questions presses against my body from all sides, an enormous vise hinged with iron clasps.

Among the questions are: stay or return? And what happens next?

Where do I find my will?

How to grab and hold on?

Love, full and powerful as a hurricane's wind, gentle as the lightest touch.

Briefly the image of a woman sitting at the edge of a bed, sobbing against an inert body—mine—flashes before my eyes. I long for her. This is pain like I have never experienced it: brutalizing and total.

Ragged shadows, some rent in places, open their mouths in silent grotesquery: a sneer there, soft smile here. The faces, if they can be described as faces, show lips moving: insistent, magnetic. Eyes unplugged, then unmovable, erecting walls between these facial gestures and words like some rancid food I cannot keep down. The woman who weeps shakes her head, waves everyone away, gathers my body in her arms. Her face is like gray rock, crossed by crevices where rough shale chips and cracks.

The questions stop walking, turn their heads, look back and pierce me with their eyes.

Now they are no longer questions but statements: perfectly round and absolutely clear.

If I turn in toward the shabby apartment, my body will be reduced to severed head, bloodied shoulders, a stump of flesh. My heart will be burdened by scars. My legacy: a statement written by someone else, repeated in my stalled breath. A destiny torn from some book of fate written long before my birth. My actions will never have belonged to me. My journey shudders like the furious water of a river crashing against rock.

Is this the same gray rock?

No, it is smooth, polished by millennia of water, standing where it is meant to stand, precisely. Salvation seems to beckon from terror's center, from that point where loss and gain are indistinguishable. I summon every whisper of will, every strength of knowledge, and turn. Something snaps, like an invisible wishbone, large as a question mark. Memory puts its arms around me, drawing me back.

Now I am rousing, struggling to breathe, returning to life beside the woman who holds me in her arms. I begin to stir in those strong arms, begin to feel once more their texture and heat. Blood rages through me, warming my parched skin. Again and again she touches me. My velveteen rabbit, I murmur, but only I hear the words. She presses an index finger to her lips, chokes on her own tears, presses me closer.

Almost lost, I hear her whisper, and try to imagine what almost means

Memories layer in any order: Marriages, both public and private. The moment she understood she needed her own workspace, that her name is Artist. When she began leaving her family's shadow and living in mine. When we got past the eight-year mark and I knew this time would be different, would not forget its name. How jealousy fled and never returned. Where trust took up residence. How Kindness became a family member, taking each of us by the hand. When we discovered, together, that only art can pave the road to that world threatening to slip between our anxious fingers.

Place writ large.

As if on a screen, moving just beyond my eyes but on which I can see its shadow figures—free of strings or maneuvering hands—a young girl leaves a breakfast table, her parents, the last remnants of tea glistening in its shallow dish, an uneaten scrap of flatbread.

The figure of another man shimmers at the edge of the picture plane. As he steps forward, I see an unwieldy vest in his hands. He holds it close to the girl's chest—her incipient breasts straining in broken acceptance, her heart thundering—his monotone of jumbled words telling a story she hears but does not understand. This is about measuring, measurement, the size of numbers but not their older meaning. Wires stick out in burning disarray. Material speaks to the girl in a language she almost remembers but ignores.

The time has come.

In this interstice of moment and place, I realize I no longer understand the mother, the father, the man with the vest. Their eyes empty, then leave their hollows of bone, fleeing a refusal to belong that tells me everything I need to know. As he fades, the man chokes on a guttural sigh.

A burst of dry thunder accompanies this brutal shift of time and place. Rivulets of pain run from my belly, along my arms, come to a sudden stop beneath my fingernails. Pools of saliva fill my mouth, then, washing away the sharp taste of fear.

I turn my head, definitively.

Looking up into the eyes of the woman I love, I begin to take my first breaths beyond such perilous escape. On the floor, one soiled canvass edge just visible beneath the familiar futon, I catch sight of the suicide vest, its bulky contour fleeing until it no longer fills my field of vision.

Without conscious thought, in the almost automatic motion I have made so many times before, the tip of my left thumb curls to push the plain gold band into the fleshy pad at the top of my palm. That ring: alive with energy. One of identical two, linked by the same date embossed on their undersides. I hear the sound of my own voice, words in the language I think I have always spoken, words that become a poem. Simultaneously I push them out into cracked air and try to keep them from utterance.

My dream fades, until only its broken contour scatters across the floor.

In a soft voice I begin to count: 0, 1, 1, 2, 3, 5, 8, 13, 21, 34. I am tired. So tired. The numbers approach my eyes, like shooting stars: sunflowers, hurricanes, galaxies. Somewhere in a distant sphere, Euclid laughs. I can see Fibonacci, prancing along the sidelines, eager to have his say.

Now color takes over. I have made my choice.

Silence pulls me into its arms. Less really does seem to be more.

With the tip of one bare toe I push a corner of dirty canvass cloth from sight, its mass of wires unruly, perhaps contagious.

For the moment I have no inclination to explain. And how would I begin, if I myself still stumble across a map that is tissue-thin, threatening to shred and scatter.

Then I saw what the calling was: it was the road I traveled.

Rukeyser's words, in my birth language and accompanied by a cello's deep tones, enter the room on a sudden wind. From the South come another woman's words: *Gracias a la vida, que me ha dado tanto.* They are more than enough. I touch the ring again and dissolve into the embrace of the woman whose face is only now beginning to lose its cast of grief.

The Future

The future, like everything else,
is no longer quite what it used to be.
—Paul Valéry

Paul Valéry said this in 1937. I was a year old. Was my future already determined, laid out like some detailed map I only need follow to be able to arrive at its mileposts? Or, as many believe, would I be writing my story as I went along? Probably not either/or. The stuff with which we're born shapes us in all sorts of ways. Still, I like to think our desires, will, and the choices we make along the way are just as important.

The Greek philosopher Heraclitus insisted that no man ever steps in the same river twice. Meaning the river is forever changing. I cannot know if he considered women in his pronouncement. Heraclitus, who lived in the first century of our era, was from Ephesus where the magnificent library doubled as a brothel. The Greeks knew how to service man's flesh as well as his mind. Women and boys, needless to say, did the servicing.

Heraclitus, by all accounts, had a number of interesting qualities. Diogenes, whose biographical texts that allow us all these years later to glimpse something of the philosopher's life, wrote that he was from a royal family but abdicated the throne in favor of his brother, preferring to live a life of study. And that he was basically self-taught, something that right off the bat endears him to me. Although preceding Socrates by a generation, he favored questions as a route to knowledge, constantly asking them of himself. He lamented the mess that statesmen made of his world, and some referred to him as the Weeping Philosopher. Little seems to have changed. I too weep at the way most leaders lead.

But I am interested here in individual lives, mine and others, as components of the weave that determines our social fabric. I have long been intrigued by the old nature/nurture conundrum. Which of our choices and decisions are determined by social class, race, gender, sexual identity, how we were raised and where, the opportunities or limitations that appeared without our bidding? And which are determined by what we create for ourselves?

Those who know me best say I am possessed of an inordinate drive. Some have described me as "a force of nature." I suspect it isn't always a compliment. At eighty, by some counts I might be called successful, since I decided early on to be a writer and have more than a hundred published books; wanted to know the world and have traveled widely, visiting North Vietnam six months before the end of the war and living in several other countries during times of profound turmoil and change. I have wanted to be a mother and have four extraordinary children, ten grandchildren and a great grandchild. I have sought enduring love, and for thirty years have enjoyed a deeply fulfilling intimate relationship.

There are also those who would laugh at the idea that my life has been successful. My many books have never earned enough for me to live on. Several previous intimate liaisons failed, and my children were conceived with different fathers. I hold no university degree, nor will I leave anything but courage and values to my progeny. But then, success doesn't reside in the eye of the beholder, but in that of the person enjoying it, or not. I feel immensely fortunate, grateful for the people who love me and privileged to be able to get up each morning and write.

My road wasn't straight or narrow. My white upper middle-class origin endowed me with good nutrition, healthy bones and teeth. My parents had three children, and we are quite different one from another. Of my siblings, I took the route less traveled. I have the poorest formal education and, by the standards of those who determine societal rules, have lived the "craziest" life. I have traveled to places others considered dangerous, and engaged in activities deemed inappropriate by the social mores of my time. The loss of beloved comrades often haunts me, especially when closing my eyes cannot erase their dead faces.

After a semester of college, I found the university courses I was offered in the suffocating 1950s to be boring and irrelevant. I quit school and, wanting to escape my parents' loving but disconcerting home, did so in the only way possible for a young woman of my class and culture: I married. My young husband and I bought a motor scooter and headed for India. Our money ran out in southern Spain, where we got jobs and stayed for a year or so. The marriage foundered, though, and we divorced a few years later.

I wanted a child, and got pregnant in New York City, intentionally and on my own. Out of wedlock it was called back then, with few questioning the "lock" in wedlock. Marriage hadn't worked out so well for me, so I decided to go it on my own. I gave birth to my son Gregory in 1960, when single motherhood was burdened by social stigma and the word illegitimate had only recently been deleted from the birth certificates of children born outside patriarchal arrangement. This didn't concern me. From the moment I was a mother I felt complete.

I lived alone from time to time and also married several men or lived with them long enough to consider it marriage. Two of those unions produced my three daughters. Years after acrimonious break-ups, these men and I are now friends, better friends than when we tried to force our relationships into marital straightjackets. Many who proclaim them-selves judges of the socially correct have commented on my "many marriages" as evidence of instability or worse. I guess they prefer couples staying together whatever the cost, like my own parents did for 62 years. I never favored façade over essence. When a relationship went bad, I tried to fix it. When that wasn't possible, I moved on.

I don't for a moment doubt the healthier route is to experiment until you get it right which, much to my joy, Barbara and I have done these past 30 years. We began our relationship when I was 50, she 35. We sometimes say we wish we had met sooner, but both know we needed all those previous mistakes to make our magical union work. Well, maybe not all the mistakes.

Early on, I knew I wanted to be a writer. Writers lived in New York City, I reasoned, and when I was in my very early twenties that's where I went. New York proved important to the development of my creative spirit, and to learning the discipline of my craft. My friends were the abstract expressionists engaged in the energy of what they called action painting, and the poets of Black Mountain and Deep Image who were writing a new American idiom. The Beats taught me about the stultifying hypocrisy of my country at mid-twentieth century, and I identi-fied with their rebellion.

In 1961, when I thought I had reaped all New York had to give an incipient poet, and it became more and more difficult raising my son in a city without social services for single mothers and their offspring, Gregory and I boarded a Greyhound bus and headed south. He was ten months old.

Mexico City was our destination. It had more green than any metropolis I've lived in before or since, a rich indigenous culture, and you could still feel the spirits of Frida Kahlo, Diego Rivera, Leon Trotsky, and Tina Modotti. León Felipe roamed Colonia Cuauhtémoc with his black beret and memories of Spain, writing poetry that brought the war for his country's soul into painful focus. Mexico welcomed refugees from everywhere. Even the country's poor had someone poorer working in their homes and caring for their children, so I had help with Gregory and got to spend a lot more time with him.

In Mexico I married the poet Sergio Mondragón and together we founded *El Corno Emplumado / The Plumed Horn*, a bilingual journal that became a venue for rebel creativity across borders. The magazine lived eight years and made history. With Sergio I had Sarah in 1963 and Ximena a year later. But his spiritual map led him toward Buddhist mysticism and mine took me to Socialist revolution. We separated in 1967.

In the United States, McCarthyism had subdued much of the previous generation, although it had produced some brave heroes in response. Perhaps I was fortunate to have come up at a time when rebellion was in the air. I know moving to Mexico gave me a vision it would have been more difficult for me to develop had I remained north of the border. For one thing, I came to understand imperialist reach by living among those who suffered its devious push and pull. Getting to know Latin American poetry was also a gift; Peruvian César Vallejo, who changed Spanish forever, had a profound impact on my own writing. Living in two languages was like having two voices, two sets of signposts on my map. Living two cultures greatly broadened my sensibilities.

Mexico itself exploded in 1968, in a fierce cry for justice euphemistically known as the Mexican Student Movement, but which in fact involved workers and farmers as well. That year saw rebellion in many parts of the world. Paris May. Young people taking to the streets in Germany, England, and Italy. New York's Columbia University and an intensification of the movement against our country's war in Vietnam. The beginning of The Troubles in Northern Ireland. An escalation of guerrilla warfare against the Brazilian dictatorship and elsewhere in Latin America. And dissatisfaction with the status quo in some of the socialist countries: Poland, Czechoslovakia, and Yugoslavia. Battles also raged in Africa and Asia.

In Mexico the government came down on the protestors with a particular ferocity because the Movement threatened the upcoming Summer Olympics. The games were due to begin on October 12. Foreign visitors were already cancelling hotel reservations, undermining the country's strenuous investment. On October 2, forces of law and order shot into a peaceful demonstration for close to five hours. The official death count was 26, but it is probable that as many as a thousand people were murdered that bloody afternoon, many of their bodies disappeared. This was my first lesson in what a dictatorial government is willing to do when it feels its power imperiled. It was one I've never forgotten.

Our magazine stood with the Movement, and I personally had also been a part of it. My relationship with Sergio had ended a year or so before, and I was living with Robert Cohen, a U.S. poet who had been traveling in Latin America looking for his own revolution. With Robert, I'd had my youngest daughter, Ana. She was three months old when paramilitary agents came to our home and stole my passport at gunpoint. Robert quit his job, we took the three older children from school, and went underground. It was clear we could no longer live in Mexico.

And so it was that in the summer of 1969 we sent all four children to Cuba while I searched for a way out of my adopted country to join them in what we called The First Free Territory of America. I had been to Cuba twice before. The Revolution was in its glory years. And the Cubans took in our four youngsters as they took in thousands of others—kids whose parents were fighting on the front lines of liberation struggles, in prison, or dead. I eventually made it to the Caribbean island via Prague, and—ill and exhausted—reunited with my family.

Thus began my eleven Cuban years. As I say, the Revolution was at its most authentic and exciting during that second decade. The great social achievements had been put in place, and the great problems were still in the future, or perhaps we failed to recognize them as such. People were energized and enthusiastic. Free education and universal healthcare were rights, not luxuries. An entire nation discussed and then passed new laws. No crime, no drugs, and safe streets where our children could play. As a poet and writer, I reveled in the fact that creative people had jobs in our fields—I worked in book publishing—and many were on state stipends simply as artists and writers.

People have sometimes marveled at my "happening to have been in the right place at the right time." I reject the idea that it was happenstance. I was interested in systemic change, the sort that replaces exploitation with new models of political and social interaction. I sought out places where such experiments were being made. I was passionately involved with them as an artist, as a mother raising young children to embrace values that mattered, and as a human being profoundly angered by injustice.

During my last year in Mexico, a surge of powerful texts by women had come from the United States and western Europe; and feminism found its way into my consciousness. I began to understand that the problems I endured as a woman weren't personal shortcomings but social ills, born of patriarchy and nurtured by capitalism. The Revolution meant big changes for Cuban women, although the Cuban Communist Party didn't see gender as a political category, at least not while I lived in the country. Institutionalized racism was also attacked within the revolutionary paradigm, but racist attitudes persisted. I was beginning to learn how entrenched social privilege can be, and that it would take a great deal more than economic justice to create lasting change.

In 1980 I went on to Nicaragua. The Sandinistas—the true Sandinistas, not the imposters who govern that country today—had just taken power, and I was intrigued at the possibility of experiencing social renewal among people who'd won their freedom twenty years after the Cubans. A lot had changed in those twenty years. Feminism was an international force. Vatican II had brought important changes to the Catholic Church, and several priests were Sandinista leaders. Nicaragua was also a country with a living indigenous population. I knew the traditional social problems would present themselves differently there, and the solutions would also be different. And so I moved again. Ana was ten years old, and accompanied me. Ximena finished high school and caught up with us the following year. Gregory and Sarah opted to remain in Cuba

I have written a great deal about my life. My childhood which included sexual abuse at the hands of my maternal grandparents. My time in New York. My eight years in Mexico. My decade in Cuba. That profoundly moving trip to North Vietnam. My almost four years in Managua. My return to the United States in 1984, and the U.S. government's deportation order the following year. I don't want to repeat myself here, but a general outline is needed to round out the story I want to tell.

In 1967, living in Mexico and married to Sergio, I had acquired my husband's citizenship, making it easier for me to work. At the time, I had tried to retain my U.S. citizenship, but had been told I had lost it. In 1985 this made it possible for the United States government, invoking its 1952 Immigration and Nationality Act, to order me deported, claiming that my writing "went beyond the good order and happiness of the United States." The truth was, the United States did not look kindly upon a woman who wrote favorably of life in Cuba and Nicaragua, and opposed U.S. policy in Central America and Southeast Asia.

Following a hearing in El Paso, Texas, my request for adjustment of immigration status was denied. I was given 28 days to leave the country but opted to stay and fight. I had tremendous support, organized by the Center for Constitutional Rights, a legal rights institution that for the past thirty years has been defending activists in every arena of struggle. In 1989 I won my case, with full reinstatement of citizenship.

In the right place at the right time? I don't think so. It's about understanding that we are endowed with certain basic human rights, and being willing to fight for them. Living conscious lives, we take what we have and make those lives what we want them to be. The journey is the destination.

Trusting my instinct and taking risks are writ large on my personal map. I don't buy the idea that instinct is antithetical to logic. Instinct and logic complement one another. Patriarchy and capitalism try to force us to choose one over the other, just as society may offer us a limited number of choices rather than urging us to look for others, ones better suited to our needs. Memory is also essential: learning how it has been taken from us, collectively and individually. Learning to retrieve and use it. Quite literally engaging in the ongoing task of remembering our names.

I didn't spend a lot of time pondering taking my ten-month-old son to Mexico. I didn't struggle with the decision to go to Cuba when life in Mexico became impossible. I didn't think twice about moving on to Nicaragua, and instinctively knew when it was time to come home. Once here, I wasn't going to let them banish me without a fight. And I was immensely grateful for the support I had in that fight. Had I lost, I wouldn't be here today. But I would be somewhere else: sharing my life with Barbara, reveling in my children's achievements, excited by grandchildren and great grandchildren, looking closely, listening intently, and continuing to shape a future.

As I reread this, I see I've emphasized my creative energies and determination, and failed to mention my weaknesses. Like everyone, I have many. I battle fears and phobias I must work hard each day to keep under control. I won't even name these here, revulsion invading my cells and terror threatening my throat with its damp hands. This is hard.

People tend to think I am entirely comfortable in the world. Not true. I am at ease speaking before hundreds or even thousands, and increasingly timid when it comes to meeting one or two. As years pass, I seem to become more reclusive: like a shrinking hermit in her small studio. Yet moments of contact and exchange continue to excite and move me, time with those I love and the discovery of new ideas feed my still hungry spirit.

My ordinary interactions are punctuated by impatience. I am beside myself, often to the point of rage, and sometimes hold others to unfairly high standards. And much deeper, farther inside, tapped down like the pungent tobacco in my father's pipe, is my personal quota of racism, classism and sexism: ills with which almost everyone in this society is born and against which we must do battle.

I keep reminding myself: it's never too late to change, to turn another corner or walk in a new direction on my map. But there are also some things that can't be changed: too long ago, too late. Some of my children tell me I spent so much time and energy trying to make the world a better place for all children that I often ignored my own. If I could go back and do it again, I would spend more time with Gregory, Sarah, Ximena and Ana. Their childhoods went too quickly and cannot be retrieved.

These errors and inadequacies often taunt and shame me. But I know that shame itself is an adversary designed to bring us down. I still struggle with shame. I believe it is our biggest obstacle to health.

One more thing. Knowing what I know now, I would have asked more questions of those I admired, and accepted much less at face value. I'm not talking about that intellectual exercise that tries to present itself as devil's advocacy. Too often that is fence-sitting or, worse, a lack of the courage needed to act. No. I'm talking about those questions too often ignored in the context of blind admiration or fear. As Heraclitus knew, there can never be too many questions.

So, what about this individual map each of us follows, this striving for a conscious life?

I still feel I am in the right place at the right time. As future becomes present, place and our response to it are what shift.

Acknowledgments

Some of these poems were first published in *Café Solo, Bombay Gin, Live Mag, Local Knowledge Mag, Truck* and *The Rag Blog.* The title poem, "The Morning After," appeared with poems by other poets responding to the January 2017 presidential inauguration in anthologies published to coincide with it: *Resist Much / Obey Little: Inaugural Poems to the Resistance* and *Truth to Power;* and in Spanish translation in *Revista Casa de las Américas,* Havana, Cuba. Others appeared in Pam Uschuk's *Cutthroat* and John Roche and Jules Nyquist's *Beatlick Press and Jules' Poetry Playhouse Publications* (volumes *Hers* and *Trumped*). "I Cannot Speak for the Gun" first appeared in *Radical Imagine Nation.* "Call and Response" was posted on the wall beside the art piece by Jonathas de Andrade that inspired it at SITE Santa Fe's biennial exhibition "Site Lines, New Perspectives on Art of the Americas: Much Wider than a Line," 2016. I also want to say here that for many years I have had the good fortune to count Bryce Milligan as friend and publisher. I have particularly appreciated his editing skills during the preparation of this book. His wise suggestions have helped me reshape several of these poems, making them better than they were.

About the Author

Margaret Randall is a feminist poet, writer, photographer and social activist. She is the author of over 100 books. Born in New York City in 1936, she has lived for extended periods in Albuquerque, New York, Seville, Mexico City, Havana, and Managua. Shorter stays in Peru and North Vietnam were also formative. In the 1960s, with Sergio Mondragón she founded and co-edited *El Corno Emplumado / The Plumed Horn,* a bilingual literary journal which for eight years published some of the most dynamic and meaningful writing of an era. Robert Cohen took over when Mondragón left the publication in 1968. From 1984 through 1994 she taught at a number of U.S. universities.

Randall was privileged to live among New York's abstract expressionists in the 1950s and early '60s, participate in the Mexican student movement of 1968, share important years of the Cuban revolution (1969-1980), the first four years of Nicaragua's Sandinista project (1980-1984), and visit North Vietnam during the heroic last months of the U.S. American war in that country (1974). Her four children—Gregory, Sarah, Ximena and Ana—have given her ten grandchildren and one great-grandchild. She has lived with her life companion, the painter and teacher Barbara Byers, for the past 29 years.

Upon her return to the United States from Nicaragua in 1984, Randall was ordered to be deported when the government invoked the 1952 McCarran-Walter Immigration and Nationality Act, judging opinions expressed in some of her books to be "against the good order and happiness of the United States." The Center for Constitutional Rights defended Randall, and many writers and others joined in an almost five-year battle for reinstatement of citizenship. She won her case in 1989.

In 1990 Randall was awarded the Lillian Hellman and Dashiell Hammett grant for writers victimized by political repression. In 2004 she was the first recipient of PEN New Mexico's Dorothy Doyle Lifetime Achievement Award for Writing and Human Rights Activism.

Recent non-fiction books by Randall include *To Change the World: My Life in Cuba* (Rutgers University Press), *More Than Things* (University of Nebraska Press), *Che On My Mind,* and *Haydée Santamaría, Cuban Revolutionary: She Led by Transgression* (both from Duke University Press). Her most recent nonfiction works are *Only the Road / Solo el Camino: Eight Decades of Cuban Poetry* (Duke, 2016) and *Exporting Revolution: Cuba's Global Solidarity* (Duke, 2017).

"The Unapologetic Life of Margaret Randall" is an hour-long documentary by Minneapolis filmmakers Lu Lippold and Pam Colby. It is distributed by Cinema Guild in New York City.

Randall's most recent collections of poetry and photographs are *Their Backs to the Sea* (2009) and *My Town: A Memoir of Albuquerque, New Mexico* (2010), *As If the Empty Chair: Poems for the disappeared / Como si la silla vacía: Poemas para los desaparecidos* (2011), *Where Do We Go From Here?* (2012), *Daughter of Lady Jaguar Shark* (2013), *The Rhizome as a Field of Broken Bones* (2013), and *About Little Charlie Lindbergh and other Poems* (2014), and *She Becomes Time* (2016), all published by Wings Press.

For more information about the author, visit her website at www.margaretrandall.org.

Colophon

This first edition of *The Morning After*, by
Margaret Randall, has been printed on 55
pound Edwards Brothers "natural" paper con-
taining a percentage of recycled fiber. Titles
have been set in Bernhard Modern type, the
text in Adobe Caslon type. This book was
designed by Bryce Milligan.

On-line catalogue and ordering:
www.wingspress.com
Wings Press titles are distributed to the trade by the
Independent Publishers Group
www.ipgbook.com
and in Europe by Gazelle
www.gazellebookservices.co.uk

Also available as an ebook.